Terrain Seed Scarcity

PETER LARKIN was born in 1946 and has been Philosophy & Literature Librarian at Warwick University for many years, with research interests in ecocriticism and in postmodern theology. He also runs Prest Roots Press with its commitment to affordable fine press work. He has contributed to *Reality Studios, Fragmente, Parataxis, Talisman, Shearsman, Inscape, Salt, Terrible Work* and *Angelaki* and appeared in *Ten British Poets* (1993). Among earlier works not collected here are *Enclosures* (1983), *Prose Woods* (1985) and *Pastoral Advert* (1989).

Terrain Seed Scarcity

POEMS FROM A DECADE

PETER LARKIN

SALT

PUBLISHED BY SALT PUBLISHING
PO Box 202, Applecross, Western Australia 6153
PO Box 937, Great Wilbraham, Cambridge PDO CB1 5JX United Kingdom

© Peter Larkin, 2001

First published 2001

Printed and bound in the United States of America by Lightning Source

Typeset in Swift 9.5 / 13

ISBN 1 876857 08 0 paperback

SP

1 3 5 7 9 8 6 4 2

Non sine si modo pro

Contents

Introduction to this Edition

We know about scarce things, they are all around us, not scattered so very much but simply persistent enough not to be primary or dominant. They assist us towards a landscape of non-insistence. This is not a place out of the way of the oppressive so much as the difficulty of the places we know which, while not being merely residual, lack any tenor of perfect or dispersive abandonment. Scarcities like this fix on a poetry until it comes to be haunted by the idea of what scarcity might be on behalf of, as a way of spending 10 years in the world: this has been most of my writing of the 90's. Scarcity as an unconditional re-emerged for many of us after ecology rescued it from being only an economic effect, but scarcity in the West remains inseparable from a notion of damage. The sense of the scarce also continues a motif in late modernism, which itself had eked out the more ancient thread of a spirituality of reversals, which in this case are slight enough to become the encounters and re-attachments subversions are not. But for me pronouncing a scarcity in what is needed to sustain life both physically and spiritually has been firstly a poetic argument, a way of getting something to appear and ramify in poetry. Such a scarcity is exploratory and speculative simply by being the lesser result or diminished arrival of what is, nonetheless, expected and recognised by us, but it is not a fixed term of mourning. If a thing is scarce it's there, rare for contemplation and happening for praise. Perhaps it might be the natural or spiritual world answering human desire with some offer of its own, one which feels slight because it *must* be taken up. And if that offer of belonging (within a manner of scarcity) to a world desired can't be written out as an absence, then it must be opened up to by means of an array of lesser differences. To be insufficiently with what is given to us is not to be detached from it: it may be a token by which to experience the unbrokenness of roots (along a specifically historic etiolation) through and towards a common landscape. Scarcity is then free to emerge within poetry as the finitely hospitable horizon of rarity and mystery; as the condition through which desiring a world magic can be made fruitful, or be its preliminary seed of contemplative devolvement. It is a turn through the initiatory blindness of root towards a scarcely representable gesture of dedication (never to be fully embedded in any material text as such, and so another lesser presencing). Because that dedication exists on behalf of a plenitude made availably slight to the gifts of nature and origin, it is unbrokenly tenuous, or tenacious where broken at the horizon's sacral wedge: yes, *that* fragment.

May, 2000

Author's Note

This collection brings together the complete texts of six chapbooks published between 1992 and 1998, together with two new texts never published in their entirety before (*Whitefield in Wild Wheel* and *Spirit of the Trees*) which date from the very end of the decade. I begin this collection with eight poems from *Scarce Norm, Scarcer Mean* (1992), the volume in which the preoccupation with scarcity first surfaced. Also included are the original introductions or accompanying essays (shortened in some cases)which may or may not be useful to a reader, but which are offered as a way of sharing some of the self-interrogations I found consoling at the time. My way out could be a reader's way in.

For their stimulating feedback and support over the past ten years or more I would like to thank Bruce Andrews, Charles Bernstein, Paul Buck, Tom and Laurie Clark, Simon Lewty, David Marriott, Anthony Mellors, Drew Milne, Tom West and John Wilkinson, and I also thank Anthony Barnett and Paul Green for typesetting or publishing involvements with some of the original texts.

For the present collection my grateful thanks go to John Kinsella for suggesting it and to Chris Hamilton-Emery for help with collocating and editing the texts.

From Scarce Norm Scarcer Mean

(1992)

i

Call for mere entropy induced
bargate off intensity of access
solar wave more floe than stock

the choke at the environmental sink

renewable is no non-scarcity

If friction isn't recyclable
its complexity 'within' supplants
a greater win to fall, atomic
change of attachment evenly scarcer
                    from full

Engineer nature in non-
mutual control, the scarcity phases
of spoil, more new loan types?

Where will one park to waste?

ii

Performances of nature alike, the amount to get it to do

    To set a grange wholly onward beside rarestander
    solitude like an arrear of number upon scarcity

Facticity already the period street of . . . interior
or neaping whether given us despite green of less

    in a giantism there we have our waver
    upon pure-spot not to incur common-otherwise
    than aspect of scarcer material

    unrare as the child liking out these weeds
    in choicest concrete, scarce our nature
    a species-followant signs in file

Of which these are relatives of the so poor reachable

iii

Scarce of means ubiquitous, what
sweet thrown noise to the frangent offgoers of place

Allotments seed a smaller by quantity
from mean product to allotment of scarce

Stationary a state given way toward insult of thirst
fondly warded with strict angling for the necessity of it

    long unglad homogeneous, not to good of refuge
    but its admittance, immobile tie
    at the rake unvitiated

    a disutility of incomparable dwelling
    intervene abode into nature

    at the meek of a fitness detriment

iv

Aggressed at resource, no prize in variables of scarcity
   intercomic purity depends from a cultic dens-
   ity expugned by reward, the shavings subcast

   The pure is stemmed with valve, clean infoliate
   to quell equivalent of entire world weight

For disabundant pure, limited tread in risk support

From unshorn opportunity leave the site scarce-adorned

v

As contemporary a litter the there of it
wherever in domus decline adaptables
as a lame anomaly climate
was history in irrespectives

Is there anything I do in earth-savings?
geoprolific to chided site

    ancient vextures of receipt
    firmage left gathered

    wisdom of set weariness
                       spells
    no reduct=no donation

    the mortal sort whose deftness
    will harbour irreplete

A cone of relations upon what rarely scarces:
loss of computation of that complexity
so inexactly blown in simples spare

To but knack perfection its most slighting
vouch: bound in sole unnegotiable
as is present in not enough

    strewn in arguant sactuary

    lap the technics ply
    prime bringings squat

    too few to reckon not

vi

Merit by attaching goods, a limit-hunt at the possible
the rest is defensive worth, a stake into protections'
upright at an effort of satiation, roofic hurt

What is nature worth has no means to the instruments

Liberal to earth but sparing in festival it fits
a field weak to world-hold, scintilla-old

It is not for nature to evolve *into* conservation
abundantly difficult to protect from universals of green

Earth's missionary expiry too laden to desynchronise
reproach as peak, extinction might be 'optimal'
    were it not an offsite mitigation
                        to spend origin
    in the object of approach
    unlendable solace scarce forcing forth

vii

Privatory stuff off roundel formation: fuel
the traumatic neatheap to its regenerate
few solutions: plentiful furtives of relief

Root affective nonaffable, unbrutals to now
of cluster, a docked scarcity rudely a plant-
ation of enough, thinned suffusively to, to
nip meanness of storm, lie on weal

Strike it gone shelter, aspective-listless
and fear environs spent in the thicket
the address not in scope of disaffection
wheresoever dumped at least is un-
triggered with the ruin ceasing
in deadly lending season

Roots in retroset
aver decks to surplus leaning.
Differ well of it and suspend
technical into numinous odds
to use so sparse a litter of the scatter.
A reception blade a narrow with, not for:
absence enough for the signal
spoil writes the least field upon
loss: if the web intrude asset
of the crossing it pools to
the scarce to be of that

viii

As property group competitive exclusion
does only finishing work; simply relax
primal having is piece-wise digression
confounding within-group monoculture
as *uncommenced is* a loom not in-
efficacious, not unhistoried return
(hastened) to no-owned but stony
locatory, torn astride a grace
lit into continence

The exactly salved stuff an ecology
of smoke, counterdrift to it dis-
missed, the reach that is in small
packets an insect on the future
as asset to non-assortment, the toll
of irreversibles so human on animal:
post-formal supplies of dependence

Additional Trees

(1992)

Should this shameful trace on the canvas of a branch that was drawn in the 'wrong' place be deleted? Better leave it. A second look is likely to discover that there is indeed another branch, just there, to justify it.

I found that the branch existed to begin with in a zone of lateral uncertainty, a vibration more apparent than the branch itself.

When at least one is entitled to a kind of certainty that at the heart of the disturbance there is a tree.

LAWRENCE GOWING

Green tree of severance
Green tree girdled against splitting

SUSAN HOWE

Tending : Prolepsis

I

Diverging *from* revision as much as from any pure vertical, it dilates its surmount and branches its non-coincidence. Addition the supplementary appendage or stabilising make-weight that *affords* scarcity as origin, a slightness meaner than the sleight of autonomy. So no autonomy of revision but fidelity to the scarcely given.

II

The overhang that adds *from* scarcity, a jointed supplement ascending through swerves to the lateral (to its outbreach), but lateral only as the followed outshare of origin.

III

The addition, those ramifyings of what there is for scarcity to be among, upon, the equable shelter of little. Addition here doesn't increase but ramifies the inclusiveness of the scarcely ordained. Scarcity is to addition what branching is to generosity. To ramify is to oppose in the mode of fidelity, not revision. The addition both provokes an opposition onto the (groundless) amplitude and renders any such forking from scarcity shelterable.

: in trying to prove it a general conjecture you start well with the corresponding result for a tree: our objective is to show how branch-bound that is, by any horizon ring

trees at the starter series

expressible branching-time

its bravest of sporadic group

: a quantum of roof requires whatever the upright: abandoning a comfort long-envied but holding to the cope: where the dangers of it spreading upon ourselves are swollen by empathy: from indurate earth to nomadic hard-over, at least wicker the perfection crosses its stood sill but finds the branch uncentrist at that

: each contrary execution path is bounded by branch: what is posed to the total of all paths is a relatively weak measure of complexity, wrong in subgoal but exciting the lightest fork of dependency: merging trivially both invariants concede *both* to the fork, an idiom or –dom without least heap at the turn

: the damage ascertained considers an independent actor: to fork from listening isolate as from banging society, further neighbour thunder not unguided but knocked through per branching-strike

: having no recognition of its own injuries it branches from every point remittent, a burden alighting to remoteness: usual origin and cause of the first branch-away, in a risk of probal ground

: bond-ex and feasible, as such an initial basis of slack variables *being* feasible: stationarity verges the exception leanest to canopy, a weakness of result embraces an expense of branching the rate

: a reel's finicky fugal under any unsagged load, mimic mutants for spindly abundances of the field, i.e. the heuristic stretch amply ignores a lack of reach forked on compacts

: at low-loss power whose dividers (blind-steady) gain colli-sional widths in the stimulated branch: minor characterisation appends undirected branch-greens, a fork of mantle to spreadlock prediction

: conservant in its disperse-to-branch, the width of path on wish beside no width of *area*: array this path across the open as one strand less its pure diffusion, open one less than: the tree's unfulfilled scatter

: anomalous branching of the common: tree-bounded disorder cissoid as a totality flown to division along infinite branch where you have no cusp 'between' procession and accession but fork at the 'in ordinary' a serve to go: reverts this weak cut-point along heredi-tarily unicoherent continua

goodness of split
a nearest neighbour rule

: roles of divergent branch as if to curve at any meta-cleavage: signed on path it might be a gradual through-branch but it does not *pass* as such: this careful division is not an embrace but only a symmetrical obliquity doubled to remaining beside

: the emptiness problem is undeniable for domains of upwardly trenchant formations but the higher alterity is not disconnect: difference soars out to a lateral of the hierarchy but such deforms spur accommodation, i.e. the branch with which to swerve is at the even for its area

> core prone off periphery
> but no *marginal* circuit

: if ramified then less subject to the paradox of self-application: no evidence against the gap as first resort but inclining turbulent-assentive: a stateless filler on the hypothesis of fractional assumption

: branching to the statics is co-sprung across a drift of middling exception, its codeviance already not *the* difference: sumptuously it has not followed that grid before end but branches onto each soonest repletable terminus

> confocal positive branch
> upper limit of absolute fraction

: rather than uncountable antichain, suppose the family of all branches has no greatest element other than its accords of dual jab: the range not embedding the divergence but branching pairward at a common surpassing, a tree to its better *lower* bound: the latticing tonal shelter as if unpalmed but myriad, as though a centre improves *that* problem

> each growth contour is twice mem
> bered of its gap in the predecession

:   branches multiply at the parting by infinity: their tracery isn't resistance but a truce of conductible passes fended over the sliding stake

> open only as ramified
> latch at void is branch
> off intermutation

:   the difference in the function not to be a difference in the element but an irreflect of divergences enwooding the distortion

> denied the departures
> but implied in torsion
> a fork bends to no plurality

:   regions don't intersect at the branch, rather forking staggers the sector of regimes: each distance stems from its own broken difference, travels to its own arcing throughout the convention

:   a parallel but nonidentical swerving: not from the centre but of its indirection to square: the branches bend low to non-death but turn to the strings of presence they go outside

> manifold sortal
> a consort at the fork

:   a tree can't know a circuit, its non-retour (as branches beam its non-tower) is not desertification amid grade but a cursive stem, a bowing of divergence over and over: the unreturning of non-drift, the quadric stance in beat of branch

> decision-tree model
> on errant select
> unspent at face

:   a convex of some branch of the recall, nondegenerate while intervals of form drip from the uniquely connected, in the manner of the span of dendritic case, the obtained topologies

:   as with looped doors danced against their aspersion, trees don't soak but shed the openness upon an elongation drawn off hazard: to the liminal pendant, shelter-form of its averting shower
dynamic of the working point
on the quailing branch

:   or any component that is branched, the follow-on (a discontinuity) holds as pairwise disjoint: no influence of parent branching at each intersect other than a ratio of orders whose measure is conditioned on non-transparency, non-extinction: however synthetic with becoming, these junctions at splice are not migratable

:   quitting on iteration-count, the next descent is at its least-distance programme: tree-procedure is only one-step optimal, no clearance overall nor any direct branch to the circling difference
at each joint of branch
that number of sources from exit

:   environmental 'correctness' is little more congenial than our own conceptual homopause, the liability we have otherwise been used to do without: whatever is degraded has the advantage of a branch before cursory hazard: and not only a system in which inanimates are considerate

:   a sufficient condition for branching in a random environ-
ment is to grow like the introduct of its means: that tree parts
observe a screen of hance

:   woods for a quantity of objects as we can but few tag the
ramifics of attention: tree of wood, wood of branch, the constrained
random walk along fraction's leaf
>   fault tree pinion
>   so prior portables
>   saunter leaf to mis-
>   credential of shaft

:   and allow branchwork is not a global sufficiency but divulges
from any tax-ture the swerve might be when such fruits tended
too unbearingly towards autonomy in the sleight: let revision
cling no more than a stick's sway cumbrous in lattice upon the
ramification's nonempty stitch: as texture against suspicion not
where the tree can be stood but its becoming nonplenty of wry
origin: which will only net this uphold in addition, in the addition
branch breaks from branch: and as sparse to ground in each
crown's frequency

II

:   no tree that isn't on the instant a nonvariable though scarce of system joining any such unit home: where branch is of a family alien to tree-recognisers whose rift hedges on admission's enucleate eye

:   keel it and the trees will wade, without fullness is reef steering across that palm: lean with the handicap they have to it, of an overwound place, to add at space

:   this eased deterministic has hardly the distribution for rousal, a mildly redundant lame stick unuses any such deduction from readiness: which, the influence of the pleasure of short branches, the multiple tall sentry decomposes to a single plausible ample

:   variance in random walk may still come to be evenly applied to traps in the stand, so less as to shade the infinite leanable by trees than at least canopy to disbranch a running field's aside
                   these carrying sets
                   its diffuse assart

:   evaluating the tree from its repeated events is not locally parsimonious: a tight upper bound for path-length aims at end-fitful spanning: the forks are leaves within the field-kitty of addition
                   save an additive spectrum
                   as lesser of bounds

:   a shallow pole flattening amid zest of spread, a dis-lodge
many times above foot: whose swerving is weak from furtherance
but fulsome at the knee: neither a severance to preserve nor mere
pendant on channel: the care of this path is not at its gate
                    enticement to pole
                    park under deep branch

:   this tree of openness forks ahead of any distinguisher desti-
nation can't ravage upon also: if closures are its myriad laterals of
stays-by this is the staying out of what it is come by: staves to sever-
ance as strips go aproned to leaf-throw, long in swarm to a branch's
palm
                    shuttered, but by a
                    cradle of obliteration
                    put beside, by

:   the point of origin will switch out but dip departure no
neater towards an 'as absence fields it': the modernity of retrieval
lets slack quasi-orders field any forkless point across dendroid spoil:
a fractal carrying set is the branch-slide's innovatory reserve
                    at an additive absolute
                    bounded on nonstationary
                    random,
                    the chastener
                    is amplitude alone

:   horizontal curtain summons the inverse initiative of apex: it
is possible to essay in the crown quite enough avoidal combina-
tions: indivisibility of circumference (how void is trefoil) spins to
each microintersect the tree leans through
                    each limb transmural
                    its competition branch
                    three-dimensional, a
                    pair windows the singular

:   though the leafless state is a paucity there is no scarcity in
branch before quandary: each departure from symmetry is a quan-
tity in itself but which must branch from so many asides: the goad
is shelter despite the climbing of guardians

> radial demotion as-
> cends branchwork near-
> surface residual assent

:   we, more lightly than quietly, arrive at the under-rest of
bough-length by a maximum parsimony principle: with those self-
broadening deficients pacific anomalies are next put to the spot
horizontal: when there is no accumulation of branching other than
girdling the appraisal

> as spine is indensity
> scarcity disgathers
> the few of addition

:   attachment fan-set at the branch-sickle: from the hand's
purchase contacts an addition not any of our roads of trammel,
cycling so: arbitrary to ramify latent, constant handprint of the
recessive cease-by: largest extract waned from pattern, real in the
net by more than the dividable's wing across it: less than a parting
by two in unsparable divergence if one adds clear of one that stealth
of space which is not alternate

:   nature can save contradictory strategies in simultaneous
speculation and lack all mirror of the myriad: which 'both' has this
parallel advantage but is not to be latticed across from one strength
to the other, i.e., the size of leaves?

> branch dividuation
> bower not peer

:   tree mechanism in the attempt to plot the node by the split:
its initial stop-at-split rule so as to minimise overall tree impurity:
signifies for difficulty but trees are often the dishonest result, larger
in the crown than the information warranted, i.e. don't single the
split which maximises but branch its incision: pick smaller trees so
as not to elevate the range of noisy splittance

> how large to take validity
> as the major burden
> in scaling the initial tree

:   they recess to both iterative and recursive increase, specific as
their elements are few: a variable that is otherwise never split on
the final tree: perhaps has very little to pursue in class membership
or its truth became taxed by too slight a variation from whatever
type descends as common, its courting of addition via too little was
common stock: whose slightness was error ravaged over the modes:
in trucks of lucent frame many avenues go to align the variation,
but its shades are the linehold users

> heurism of bias
> versus isolate invariance

:   trees indicative of apparent data to the extent the splits
twigged this was information a question at a reach, whether two- or
three-paired, whether bifurcated earlier than jointure, etc.: addi-
tion centres on the ramule's thin repetition of guiding appropriate
stopping rules

> dual converse where branch
> splits expression
> repletely broken-safe

:   tree-fractured regression competes for any linear session:
lights in the tree are the offpeak advanced: branches tracts whose
interpretation can be allowed into the log, a set-astride field result

: the spur to transformation is subject to few nonnegative constraints but the few that arise spare do aspire to the margin of the scope: as concretes are a sufficient weak distance to govern direct rapport at the addition's attenuants: implemented sparsity is the branch-user in large codes
reined infit to mix
erect at feasible region

: reduce until a fresh residual is tight upon addition, the contaminate-normal: frequency of variant exceeds novelty and inclines to additive: whose select wedges create no cycles
bonded branching at (as
not) bounded
the flower of addition
in lowest gift density

: recall each go-space can be embedded in lots, some as near as others: the enveloped will appear to be a good extension: hollow sphere conjugated to broad meeting in the branch, cross-like in the enter of a branch
constrains no crossing
rafted to the fix
branch at no-crossing

: that x can be embedded in the universal dendron, planable smooth or needless to enjoin its *own* embedding, but if the reversal doesn't occur at branch then no point of x has an immediate successor

: due to an extra branch of surface, this island at floor re-lies, the spectacle at large branch: fascicular topography semi-opportune of process and gentle of occlusion: to low-drive branch sealant

:   when the roots lie in splinters surface to surface, branching is the addition of what the break is 'to', encompassing filter: forked in the brightness it exiles to a wickered outbreach as might be fled the packet of encirclement: more attired than that, the branch forks *into* what otherwise can't apportion it

the recessful additive
from larch to porch

:   on sheer and intimal thickness of branch go rooted trees: if the pole's stability is avid of limb the edge set of an oriented tree is its portrait cradle, where double is aslant from nothing but the sequence trouble of the fork's parity, its single tent

bundle-branch reentrant
blocks to cessant periphery

:   deep convective envelope on the asymptotic giant branch, the pulse of addition fetching its length effect, correcting parsimonious trees for unseen substitutions that might otherwise underextend the array, however anti-similar: cells of origin were only ever simultaneous when the branches allayed their miniature durations: dormant primordia at a final mixing in extreme horizontal branch: this is but additional shelter over externals which haven't differed to divest, the ascendant noninclusions of ground whose respects it hangs over, branching

:   unrooted trees at every root window are still its compatible solutes as a frankness in relic branches from repetition: the portioned grammar regaled from what packager's tree?: this going across axial harbour a ground will furnish by finishing (not as it shoots to termination, but where all may lateralise above) hangs out its fetters of branching volume, the refraction added

:   no-one expects the tree to go the way of its branches: at a clutch of difference it is rather to fork an inactive hindrance, or agile source as engageable obstacle diverting the crown to less than a parallel: to be less than born of branches but still what it must refuse of apex: if it there divides to its lateral appointment this neighbourhood with origin is at a less than stolen advantage in the less, any ingenious small matter of branch: a tree is uprooted all by itself widening to shelter: this lessness, localic patch topology, to be branched at the displacement where not: the conserve of fork: so the tree thorns itself into openness casting through the textures of implement: what fills to divergence the holding tool of apartness, branch-fall

> though roots mayn't burst earth
> leaf will lattice a span that has

:   as leaves prevent branches rerooting, alerted from fund to shelter: at each fork a residence corrected but accompanied, ill on course to stay hard by foundation, the indured upright may straggle into whatever branch it exserts and can expect: monolayers from the graph, polydisperse as mere muster to know a breadth of the biform

:   branch pattern succeeds only as modified to fall closer to a point laid down later, occurs as open one delay only in all ports of the tree, including tree-dimensional rootnet: rootedness in another not merely as transition *from* root but the encyclical of a form that has only branch to end in, whether no longer surface but its vestment or not (root to bend in): root is precisely absence at the prompt to which it hooks, round which it tucks out of subject-hold: retention without return but 'staying' always broader: this partial loss of access to the mode of constraint is reckonable if the blank is appeased as an arrest: no lessness-to-model need heed, for this has only 'done the round' as branch may not: as *it* may then relegate any generosity of presence, knot for notch

> the root of tree has no parent
> ascends, not rescinds, dependents,

                    depth of nesting to an
                    equivalent branch quota

:   how to brace a one-narrative tree, paracompact, in the thirl of
closed images of go-spaces, so to induce infinitely many decrements
for the ranking root: the down face must pluralise but all
constrained wefts are feasible, fitting methods on the least absolute
evenness into following block
                    usual matter to lure the restriction
                    'no meeting of nonterminals'

:   the nesting of extended states is not proud but very little
branch-wise: all those notions of a fair abroad are only conditions
on paths so far as the branch: simplified trees are but average to
abnormal addition, the hope of any enumerating bower on the
stretch: irreducible if all its leaves are labelled co-parture at branch
point

:   the average size of *reduced* trees satisfies at an urban-horizon
future, narrative as minutely concrete as it scarifies the stand
                    fewest notes down to component
                    subcontinuum at a dendron
                    to border the shade by zeroes
                    subtract to root an initial how
                    steady in branch, path
                    subject to tip-deflect
                    idealise a fast from cycle
                    in erect branching sponge

: the sole ascension a vertical becomes is the scansion of hanging fork: there it is unbroken to overhang and comes to a part in the branch: so welcome a reach-training, it gathers the selectivity we crave (a myriad if not to use all the unbroken) and flatly shelters all our purgers beneath: an effect of least-grounding to the extent, quite unsevere of swerve, a quaver upon the lack of accent: a leaf if it is the last element on a finite path

: with embrace unpricking clasp, by avoidance and surround its globe become skeletal to horizontal as lateral limbs are farther to fewer: holds the branches' re-ensuing opponent on the terminal portion

III

: whatever the loss ratio is to the source, the conspicuity of finding it out at network is finite: not the sufficient but the scarce in addition: this consideration of least effort rides the branchings

: solely a globalism of tryst-dissonance, the salience treed to sector keeps the affect arboreal, commonly bundled as unnatural except appropriated at less than own datum

: wanted—stronger branch-ties on nonpoint source, at least a surge whose genial deviance defers to the tanglewood of unengrossed command: not procured but alleviated in branch in a rareness of origin as ally

: the base may be empty inasmuch solely a unifiable-occupiable: to packet-unify, instead of raising to clash-failure, names its break-cycle not in falling but in branch

: tree unification strong enough to offer dependence of concrete variables, but weakly restrictable if no variable can instantiate a nonvariable

: hidden for concrete or the variable at whatever congruence is no generality of tree, but what there is to add to any unifier, the completeness as a less-between subtracting to a tending, branched among

:   after the initial merge only the newly producing fragments sail by branch, as how a sparse array *finds* without any updating of base: that any variable so dependent accedes to the pathos code-extra to base

:   the surface is never so random we can afford its sourceless-ness, but is the keener to be enveloped in the toss or ricket of impartings

:   where the random is eclected to centre, its completion less site simplifies additional periphery: no void is insular where its disturbances are branches

:   the great tree whose solitary axis outweighs the focal attach-ment of the world: whose non-bifurcating branch exerts into the hollow of o and does not change sign: whose higher branches have but a single turn, oscillatory or ashake at a fixed amplitude of departure: to infinitise half-branches without turns

:   a method not of proving limit but of branch-dragging a discretion of the arisen in the radical wild

:   two branches from one stem, constrictor response set at parallel elongation: at each branch content an endgroup counter-atom: the bower of nondeterminism in polybranched bounded case, the width of scarcity's addition
> pliants across multiple refirms
> sacral poor in sold divergence

: explode a tree palm-like in its prehension of hazard, see that not every equivariant ramifies finite to group in manifold: but no unfolding time during a search for unique tree without impetuous hierarchy decisions

: specific to multitude whose terms of face the network panders border as just those of the average case, a forest of listing informations coronal at chart: moderation full of pattern but across intrinsics of least effort: artificial but bi-entering, this 'local' enlists a scant nonbasic to centre branch which then enmasses to enter basics

> determinism's angel
> the sect at deplete posit
> non-deter-unison

: cue the underhang of the branch-swept tree, the decision between borne and unborne, the ledge of innocents, or a tree that sheds its own ascension to the forking, an arc of haven in veer of toil

: if compassion doubles choice by merely branching it, it amounts to a more decisionless local-bind than here: as having fronted both gates, you stay, not just suspended, but branched against the entire cycle

: trees fly of the the earth, not off the airs: out of their appointed array to branch the unaccommodated plane of shelter: scout and keep trees of uncountable models, their girdling of early season in alley sward width

:   but recovery of abduction by one single branch its re-nerva-
tion: this inadvertent preexistent is an induced sequel to origin: the
curve of its abstention from horizon is the immeasurable become
scarce at local remove, like any normal oscillation: the outgather-
ing of like ground, groundlessness's unlikeness to void

:   a superstrate of the full imperfection, behaves as a class of
intermittency in the disfronted component: or as branch-cut is inte-
gral when done with arising, an intransient scattering from a
perfectly conducing trunk: of no compound than this
                    unified piece-wise, cut
                    that combs the node-tear
                    these but the few regularities
                    of core-charged branch

:   hardly an environmental server for private change, or auto-
matic good as low-loss integrated Y-branch: any asides involve some
coarsening in the directory solidified: to be adventitious is no
defence, as these radiants are unusually distant acceptors

:   we are more to our behalf than needs add, we reached branch
a division ago, the half that ramifies below: what remains on site
has partitioned basis, here nothing but saturation effect from stark
shift, the accessible indisposable: trees of even distance between
non-endings

:   the faithful case: were x a tree so there must be some edge
pursued that does not branch *around*: such a tree has no definite
paths wrapping its given, rather the extreme forming of expressible
conditions: best step now may give rise to the worst possible overall
solution path

:   by strict concavity of shade, its equality holdings the elastic threshold that gets trapped at local maxima: a spare wilderness in the interests of each partition: became a non-radiative narrowly overtaken *by* junction or its moment-load *at* union

:   inside any blind-ending branch spreadzones are lifetimes of dissociative array around common relay

:   deep branching in the green line of descent, restive to salvage for blunt trauma: ramifying a tree is finite only to non-immediate successors: robust at outlyer: at heartwood a residual scarce *extends*, absolved of its heir

April–December, 1991

Seek Source Bid Sink

(1995)

For Geoffrey Hartman

. . . a natural sink in one corner of it. That was the jewel which dazzled me.
                                                                    THOREAU

Note

"Sink"—the opposite of source, a place where or process by which energy is removed from a system, or some specific component is removed from a system, either stored or destroyed.

A device whose function is to act as a sink.

A flat low-lying area where waters form a bog, or disappear by sinking or evaporation.

A scene which attracts the troth of source, in its part by sub-tracting the truth of what might be stored or destroyed of the beginnings we have for absorption.

Autumn 1992–Early Summer 1993.

I

For first passage times across general boundaries, consider earth in columns as of two soils, its start-away and sink-in. A net absorber, in open circuit, at the candour of origin.

The massable irreversive, simplifying new which is impotence in setting, a stride in sinking.

So to spike onset close-jettisoned from origin. Whose rapid turnunder in this active fraction was fidelity, quit, like a section in return bloom at the troubles of a peak of provision.

That stabs into the interior thermal drivings. Off vertical circulation such an object-start to force sinkage, with which to pile it well-of-drop over source.

Large with universal fatality which does not vacate. Releases streamed tall into risk at the merest. Revisings brook an initio steeped in sink.

These factions of source are the breakages beginning was putting down-gradient of any injection zone. The vertical shrinkage jetted the wells in beady arrangable cautions.

In situ production primary in detritus, flung at source, not yet of standing within sink.

Inauguration can't withdraw in compressible pore but is bid shunt, lust at drain in plumes of a below-source enaction. Sinking fluxes will web primary production. Deficit clusters ford cascades on the sink-strength of its radical.

A there-stem has spiral flood, inject the confined sand rude to sink the reception behind stores. The environment a warren at every-thing else. A wash of no-origin to its obstacle dearth, at sink in the hearth. Any nurse crops a considerable source of the mass.

Appertaining particles which stick to sink but hatch in no mecha-nism of their surrender. Crewed aside of the presider's contami-nant, but a sheer, the indispersibility content at its harbour of mishap.

In stroke stop in earth as though not to be frugal: as though origin is to spare alone. Universally, favorably opposed. Sink into what is to be at sanction, local claimant drained.

The simpler the earth the surer it will *abstrict* this jut with source. Put to distribute beginning, how region and origin are hunted aslake.

Rocks into the spurn enclaved and clasps it its sink. Infinite allay upstood in chute, stone opening under stone, each plummet of part an incident of adoption.

This was acceptance serve-acre at a wound, for not having room. Will cede of nurture how most reception doesn't unpack, smacks to a space which will fully fall back.

Unassignment dips encinct, at this state no injury band is more than finding abode. Whichever settlement's treason is vitiated our subduing was not its attention to us.

If spoil were not undue space, due down of it. It could only be fateless the condoning horizontal amendment, attempt on void as avoidance of vertical hold. Which would stanch the unofferable minus a sink ratio.

Localised spoiling which mends the homing structure, reminds us through insult of our credit towards sink.

Hiding this ruth at its pit of uncompliant nest. Its wound a drain to us the neutral enabler we do have given the blanch dysfunction is for falling down a measure, whose irrigational trench need not then go tenantless under increasing auger.

Select capsule of persecutory material the more induced with sink. Or vertical fluxes of sinking bulk not in trap to source but its particulate common. The furnishings found, are punished, ahead of function, so let them drop, spend more lowly the pitching precomplete.

Homing subrends any further impact. That it was not an originary quailing it is not the wrong of, compulsorily close, slowest drainshare at the survive of source.

At once we might not shirk marks shaven to the sign-have, unstraggling attachments whose spurt was to *turn* at given, a panic-touch of space-use (special us). Bunched but not bowed in void (spared in drain), never absolving the sure of void to be so hemmed by shelter.

Maps of deep sink with classical sequence of loss of low, opinings whatever a surface is taken to regarding its rank, perhaps with complaining fructal deposition off erosional beginner.

Basin of contrasection, basin of contractant furtherance, exempt lowlying of nurture shallow as a sink will be, scollop nature of its instigate globe's cycle.

The earth vestigial in tumultuous absorption only, not in any mere portion of fundless beginning. The drone of shelter into resource, renews, alludes, bestorms. Staving *onto* wound because of unmalice of affliction, strewn to fill shell with small of sink.

Brought to admit the collar of us into opening's accessful descent, by bonding breakable further than surface, *where* reachable unsalvable.

Why, it obliges in difference a dropped kind from nature as obliquity centering kind its wounding way to a combinarity of fallenness! To be received into any of the discaps, of a damaged but enhollowed, disallowed-hallowed fall full.

The sinking rent bow-thrown across a shallow drop. Subdeviants sink to fallen-new heights, descend into components that sit.

A circulation completed in the two intervals (source/sink) between condition.

Under seekable providers at surface abandonment, the earth's undesertable gibe. Dislocational sink the length of the completion, its creeping flow between source and sink in the presence of a sphere.

II

Bitterly improbable begin proven onset, infinite bite in the sunken happening of almost.

Drawing an irregularity fine from such other porous disorders, the eddy sinks into source to settle a whole pattern at a disexaction.

Within radical brackets swopped from the cleaving, a small package a cultivar from hounded envelope, curling into sink.

Drawn to a different (referent) saturation of every obstacle origined to abandon.

Accretion sediment across active margins, a limit contention or source chimney from lowest to most vowed.

What sinks is a girdle the assimilate is, less tube to soak passage than its attribute to have been harboured at some crisper transition.

Trawled by dispersers but still fetching in sink, scape of a source path has only this saline patch, evicted into pause at the sole vicinity pond.

Loss evaded by stronger sink in the disappearance, given a dormant input awakes at throughfall.

In concert with decrease but under sink-limit conditions, the shallow ditch, the drying pan, easily siphoned in and out of phantom retainers.

Horizon canopy acts as winter to the throughfall, a threshold now much less season than its stilled competition sink, the due of what descends in and out of cycle. As source crosses to sink there is rarely exception for much dipping *from* canopy, its post-antithesis to limits due filling.

The sink is no removal for origins depicting fall, but, lacking scant in the imperil effect, migration from source sends for drift in sink.

In the bottleneck the initial founder size, the source sopped up by transigent final earth's sucked finite.

No gaps too rich to detract the nonfinite intention of earth, the search of sink, shallowing without savouring the intent on down.

Deepwater if showered upon vertical shore, unbuttressed but a piled plummet to its resident shallow.

The reception bay wide enough to be sunk from dissolved fall, debris sedate to high primary ductivity snows its shallow-water flux.

Debris the simulation of source and fate, its frail fall-shape to troth. Near complete kernel loss would not have been attributed to a random initial distribution or a perfectly absorbing sink.

But there is insensitivity in unloading across the effect of elastic fields, such a floor was induced by unmerged quench, until natural vegetation sinks, not stores, the sore of the source.

The uncouplers were not heeders of waste, were not its taken but as if direct-seeded of transplant shock upon absence. Absence upon sinking: any saturable component at persistent downfall meets just such a cotransport type whose carriers are abstaining from source group.

Frequencies of resistance step at surface itself, scarcely a sample but is discrete to any sink-through: a portion of source falls then to its unamended soil-chamber. Where constant thickness was only compartmental.

Scales bow, patterns soak the fail of advice, efface the firmings of sink. As drain is from excess in its narrowly aslant a make-weight when diffusion is no longer the undoing of it, for all wiles longer a make-shift of origin.

As anything shorn of bounding pulls ahead of the rest. It becomes a bulge, then a point diffusion versus surface tension, falling slowly atward via a turbulent downmath seeking by what it incedes.

Or a supported lure in short of migrancy. The townsheets tell a world of surety under our children's tables, statics of their crowding are its roaded pool. If there is some subsidy in cave-in it may beckon the completion-hollow, as green radicals herd their easings between our beneathings.

We reaped enough of the invitation to talk terror of its provision with reply by injury: to intract (hollow into) overshoot. Other than this giving way (sink) of what was preformed of us, there arises this never to be compensation for surplus settlement: no cohost among a solitude of infestations.

Sediments toil between source and sink of the homing contaminant. Understores for nonimporting surface are sinks into singled cubicle. Are the habitat deteriorant unique to it, traced through this metapopulace laying up its date mistimed, unresigned but received in sink without the sour admissions but on the part of the reversals.

Point-source bog and fen the emitting sites, the exudate afterwards crushed and centrifuged. They compose the admittance of final waters to transient storage pool. The confining weathers between bed and pore.

The in situ sized in reparation is reduced in bane. Sinking *plus* offended particles, intact transit beyond the relative to the broad. Macroporosity resides, not decides, the input.

So skindust in flotilla does not encyst the membrane of the pool, is generalist heeder, not local (too global) neighbour. Our dart to depth will flout by soul what undulations of the kind (without under-ration) don't weed of light. By a mere's fall-mote shadow fallow through it.

Not that surface waits entrained for deepwater formation, a net heterotact may incline to either terrestrial: unbegan but taken through, or clear beginner sunken into.

Fear the wisdom of knowing what has fallen out of level, a sunken pool of no sowing, shallow lapse without immersion. But serve it within sink.

If there is fall there is injection funnel, a needle surface along proximal segment. Fast-sinking particles alight with, but do down, the plume of near-surface signal. A marked portion will have leaked into the flooding medium, until surface bitten by surface is craning for exodus but sinking *ahead* of severance.

III

Show stability a dispersal at grid in the sink habitats, a transub at some set sink of: to accumulate to fronts in failure of a similarity solution. The present patience of stationary overlapping pours the sources.

Predictive linkage, penetrant sinkage: a downcrease in long outlasts. At nonhorizontal walls a permeably stratified inferior. No pathway stimulus can falter this tissue-mimicking original to the scale of a global solid. Whose source emissions decline in the natural sinks of phantomly adjacent soil.

Detopping obtains draught on the beginning day, an aeolian dust sand from the oceanic. Trace source-to-sink noninfesting how it is with the turfs, these fall from insertion into a sheer dose-descendant .The protoperiod within the acid universe was not solely reach-up but vacuole.

Bypass flow as though under pasture of an undiscovered slit: inducement to the nonhollow of global sink. The green area due sink by seed-fill and did not annexe the duration.

Bound(ary) recedings may offer a period explanation (any) for the initiation and suggest fall-sediment is a *secondary* source.

Yields pace out their acclimation to a non-enriched assimilate, bind the relative aptitude of two rites of sink, loss and root.

Remission off origin a grade will sap fruit-control, an instillation unfed by the share condition. Measures from the steady state final-but-open to the finite initial that *reserves* sink.

A weak origin had baled out with scarcely a bobbin beside the indented abundance but reeked of instilment barely under. So far surfaces no longer bold to float plead their treachery sediments in raking curious sinkflow incipients.

Spread deposits like these minimally register as source organs, unless, with something of an inward current, the elemental loss rates a faster mass in sink

Present by virtue of sudden fractal models of world-need upon a fall-through of scale. These downcore ranges are negative but not competitive: from source branchlet to sink internode.

Whose populations acquire preferred onset latencies, reducing inward currents to transient storage pool. Between the young and the old beginnings, nesting any higher abundance of cavity-request.

The natural root of grouping. Immediately upon any occupation straddled by horizontal mission but more nearly sutured like a *vertical* pocket for the drawn nest.

Error as source lends what is not self-cancelling: a sacrificial flashpoint drones across its interminable brightened transience. Its sink is error tended, wound-sieve below wound-induced. Whose zone slipped off the flat of the observation, to a chamber whose largest internal source doesn't get dry by disaster, but shallows a soak-symptom no longer ovecome, the offer.

Ipsilateral to get spiked on sink but less any normal segregation of it. Such a percolated deficit *despite* sink is small, the local total was to remain finite only *at* a universal. For the rest the fraction lies in fundamental niche.

Do not yet imagine any large central sink (the negative peak of invoked material) *will* remonstrate the confluence of the ipsi.

Sinkholes draw themselves around the mounding pittance of sources. More densities linger within the errors of the analysis. To be out of force as source crosses to sink.

A principal dust of sources in test to room of absorption, ingesting the provisos of leave but not crushing the sinkers.

A glance stares at beginning as though to re-enoble, once held, the fruit of it: the flower clusters at stronger sinks than roots. Collected by gentle, vicariant centrifugation that the unusable bedding remains entire.

Compacts during a sleight, the period evicts into size. For which no normal compound can condition the source other than ascendant contribution: the uptake partitioned in storage unfounds.

These are daily dynamics, a mass balance of us to vindicate a common immensity of dipped courses, the advective flux in the channel weeping short falls below. Whose subduct simply cried sentiment: for low-motived biomass avid at senescence no stronger upon a relish of deform.

Dark respiration on drying mass accumulation, a late halving in splendour but kept to the source side. Sinks are direct selection that every earth-part lies with its source. Simples at unroot don't cleave willingly with the anthropogenic transients.

Creating its break of the share, not its shame of the entry-brake sheltered steered fall.

The dipstone into the pool of sink no whirl-of yet, as yet unspurned of a poor partaking among feebles not given equals.

Steeping or then sinking, like as not makes shift of the descent through a spiral empathy of path. Indismissably ducking affinity laving across the entire stealth of sink.

A void, when beyond insistence, as if pent, more in breadth to the sink of pool remaining our custom. Mere warmth is not the 'enough' of severed bonds.

Whose capillarity (a world) is unshunned in the devoid. Lack-to-place sites a fallen-to-conjoin. The sinkly wader of it, shallows more turbulent than intrinsic shorn.

No recanting storm, but discharge into the sink-holes of the conturbation has shunned any contumely that would level the avoid.

As though experimental plots were disposal *sources* and not such furtive welcomes remediate-contaminate. The expunge by pits sunk from countering. Universal earth asks to be begged partial of this generosity, as a species strike of shelter. Retention groping the sink's tremor of origin.

A still deeper relax may suggest only spoil, with what is innocent occurring at the hold of a piece of glade steady like the sink of it. Not a living product but the scansion of the living upon absorption. To maintain a chosen from the pulling aside (is pooling) of its own thread.

Possessor of natural shelter other than waiting over the bias of the tributory. No evening of source other than its sinks. Recess only what the offence is, not wound to set hand on, uphold not to relay on: may not steal a haste of sink.

Coeval strength in the present divacancies: the emptier allocation has rarely altered sink demand. Upper least bound sinks *at* hardmost lower. For all that a float-sink datum becalmed to begin *upon*, is punctually porous draining the end-entity of time either from or towards its global well. Age after age arisen is creation within liftcage, alas the short-period super-lattice.

Natural sinks of the containment, stalks in groves, is forest the missing sponge? Findings pour, are last, in lap of the unhoused urban heat-sink. Available is much park work at the translocale of foliate-applied area.

No-one weans your study of repose among shallows of stone dousing stone: the cranny of delay is soundfall which accompanies a drop-dealing rest upon yes, from origin upon 'no'.

The addiction of bulk flux, drift profiles of whom there are no collectors, but are at sink from their suspended.

Usually disjoint, the commons celebrant vows out of harmony, the sink of it perfect. All that severance could advise, not taken up, this sinking meet from a source's gainly bowable.

Though we over-inhabit the earth, we turn, oozing, to the frugality of our origin an account of it. What is reception to-be-lost, still withheld (sunk) from us.

To sink a single vertical desire through a domed world requires a flocking of horizontals, the intricate marsh of smallers. No such opportunity can be supervised by a natural danger as the enough: setting by source for risk, it is sink's settlement's danger off default.

Three Forest Conformities

(1997)

ONE: To Edge
TWO: To Line
THREE: To the Vertical

We must heighten rather than diminish our capacity to understand divisions of world space, even as these divisions shift, dissolve and reform. We must enable ourselves to think through borders without simply pretending that they don't exist: when faced with a forest, we should not simply declare that we don't 'believe in trees'.

C.L. MILLER

Whoever passes this way is bound to the tree of its gleaming and perpetual heaviness, upreached in the noises of portraits and simplicities.

T.L. TAYLOR

I

A place too savage for invalid aligning. Wayside cutaway at an infringement raggedly besetting edge, the motive holds shelter fielded a strip of error. Wandering is for the same overly things. Take a furtherance of rest where a grove guides uninsular at rewordable link: the groundless pause at groove.

Fibres are not hung out as garments at forest fringe: the very succulence draws in danger, human-indemnified in havening texture. The edge-lock's uncrushed lack.

A hem torsion than meeker switching things, perforant thicket to sustain the stab as maps go over sides, *on*tolerant healing of an effrayed inbled sill.

We are put to tree behind prompted verdure. We environ the mean kernel of nature, do what it has lost to do, or can fringe scarce-everywhere a rule of ex-exalted, -exhausted horizon.

An edge symptom which protects the earth at an against of isolation. As though the meddle of forest fields you checks in line, ensweetens its outshot with the trees' lone wedge.

Flimsy dwelling which they split to line aground, conventionless state of drawing out nest: grained by unassisted forms of the known.

the unwanted, unwarranted shoulder of tree population
a compression-wood endearment in conifer
how silent the mutation, if clearance extinct
the purposes of a detachment pine
lie more still or slow upon release

The shade stints the webs at their sides, here is no wrong in a ridding side to pinelight. A dispersion of estimation local within the depletion confers the binding. Shadows verge their frail figured bite upon a light unsmitten pledge. Oblique in trees, for those were co-firs, rose extremely close to the inhibition.

A probable cleavage site by blot, the leaf portion mistakes the opening for a looser spread of fate, but is correct at void only to each nearest edge. This disfavour trees grow by themselves, along the tether or waver of pervious alignments. Stop this for the edge: an untied thread was previously only *any* opening.

how an ante-nostalgia bristles!

stored in the sunder
copsed for want of wide

what notch as barrier was along laden area

This coursing edge with nothing to hatch but what smears the cartogenic. The family of it has no average of slope onto regression, the leanest hide of a concurrent. Bridle maps cut to transects preferring still more edges to the habit. Do not repine the blade a meadow to shadow.

A clearing may not edge a forest it has not yet depleted, its nurture at a covered ledge should not be as unspent as it is. Particle-wending at steaded barrier, the bar-carrier.

I drove, repulsed, at the given-way, so many mild trees no more than hedge height felled at their linear logics of aspersal. The outwork is a rabble at bonding: that is, backing off from as many of the other micro-courses. Tower the extremity of edge with a filter spine curt to minimal rise. That you still look over.

Forests shift, stably over what they are not low enough to shunt. To traverse a level occlines to the convention it has not been shunned to grow. Forest schemes are the unit to radical.

Badly fringe horizon forever beside, not ajar, the outline not then 'upon' but unopenly surpassed by the supposed demission it can fold over, shaded from desert into the desert it allows.

Or unforesting discretion of tree-cover. Not to infill horizon but shallower row when shadow goes downwood. Spent lengthward, there was always a doom of frittered vestment one wile less than desertion.

Not wildly diversified where there is industrious cover, but leach particles widely wooded where (spat to where) pause sets out parse. No tree which is not immarginate to a ruse arboreal in hoop, a capillary basal. In a promiscuous confinement of identities. To enshallow in shade, foreshorten the sore tops, of the privative in nature.

There rounds every such scarified sore: the first clarity of the wood. That the clearing, never to be desert, springs no nest. *That* comfort is in the filligree economy shone on find: shelter not so much an addition fringe-avid at breakdown but *raised* on edge: 'no nest not desert' is borders away from consequents, what edge-ordinary brushwood wouldn't punish an even way among givens?

The make of this origin hasn't deserted to space but trenches into the hollow fable of reversion. With space to hallow. If excess of loss (made nest) weren't shaded out, it would awe a concession of ability from the damage. A desert scolded in nest, split by its lines of fold, aligned as the nest is punctured by trees. Who should refresh a forest forcing into nest?

With what rod to establish the manners of fate? Forests are spurned to solemnise the land, when this isn't an emergence blessed where it tries for edge solely for the edge's craft. A sylvan cringe is limit not monitory research.

What is sheer to difference coped by another sharpness of what fringe there is to it, and has to steer linear and vertical when withstood so much in kind. No looser, leakier canopy than this, vile posting at the pinioned cross-over, a transition which mostly squats in its angle without any pulse to rue conversion.

A tree's permission will not simply bunch against bare-wood, it would sooner hunt the edge. Fringe is loosest forage, given some lunge. Untouzled birch shares what spreads across cut-off, but needn't make haste to its winter verticals.

The feathery fragment, fine brash inflects set chaos, the transfer links are byways through a sand minuter than the break at dust, as if a damp wind bracketted them against stock, the picket shaft. Not purging as such but their non-retort in the forecore of much.

All repeats which could be persisted in by not-owning, time had wanted done with as though frail to present some unvariable, and further blurted against this abutment a friendless transit which robbed variable of variable until nothing has passed unpossessed: no dwelling without reinforcement.

> the fullness of sect may have evolved once only
> discrepant inspection of plea to lot

Given such rim-feature, the region of the protection isn't purely mal-functioning, however dire-bedded the cluster. Collar is ribboned beneath cowl, the surround veers vacantly but under severest pull upon hooding, scarcely a mode of meek cause. Strict deadwood in such abundance is to predict foreign housing. A relay tree-to-tree noting only the sallies of trait which bend to the condition, or rend-ration, of remnant hardening.

Linear as yearly, nomadic continuity small bounds of stop where bonds perform no steps. The retiring alongward, wherever an edge besets containment temporary as any outdrop. The function of forest cover is regularity at a dandying of tribulation.

> frugal recourse to bough-end
> the fugal profligacy of edge
>
> dark reaction limes, massing the intact
> zone, but lacking barrage

edges were bramble to the bounds, surlier
than no extra protection

a nurture-drift resents mere park hedge
despite ancestral shock is clandestine
against arid, a heal-skill barrier
grasses (lashes) the open trap

With rind at the entrance, the rest is shade, some the things of pine,
selvings made jitter and stump with vestibule. Which the avenue
apart from its larch has split no more than to venture in trim, then
reduce each bole to a coder edged on point, many a tree wall-less
but a stubborn pinful. Parted naturals adjoin the pinch-flanch, it
spits needles' internity.

A standing stock of desert adjacency, sliced by trunk: prolific eaves,
a division quiet in overhang. Its apportioned gleaner travails
between green sweats of error, common up the vegetable tower, or
entailment at one more upright. Where a host place is judging not
to claim.

a stapled forestry of last year's hues
last yards turn back the gate in the path

the quip a tree stung to the attached:
convention's unbenumbing parallel

A beacon racks the construct which it merely raises, as if nurture
bids relief to it, not in deposed nature but in its grounded obstruct.
Obscure selvage, cellerage, submit the edge to involuntary promi-
nence which the trees seal but tail: the shadow of law the referent
hood they were rarely awry from, for if so they stop up the cope in
the rent. Whereas refer tear to cover.

the tool of cover knows no trespass
merely the beseech of postnudal forest

The plight of any bound day must itself nip nurture as it forays open, to any bald forward, but is only sent toward from beneath scored but appeasable covert. At intemperate fringe shade adjoins the disforested: seek any diminishable tension which does no more than quail beside.

The forest's stake-edge is her bandying such petty stuff as is ever let down on the earth's bluntest settings-out. Not to shutter the idolatry of remnants but glimpse the immodesty of shore through trees on such scab-points of used having.

    owing off forest this buyer in origin
    long speddings of dehistorical vert
    hours of lines drop and rethirst

As commonly as the desert is shadowed by its postgivens, arrivals by the fragment, idents in equivalent densities that are too much shaken until difference is no longer done in merely leaping the scales. Is this another binding transfer? Such others are squadron others, some other nearly the next turn, but driven into edge, not siphoned along margin. Nowhere else for trees to prick through for fear the liable is not yet here.

    better-wooded in the regionous gaps

    so tirelessly native, no
    balance restores to fringe

    the edge of forest exacts a fine trespass

II

Trimming any derelict way if trees are not to be distributed. Their ranks inch through what a siege deports, they only bridle line at like restorations of inattention. Because there are no deflected trees. None so intrepid as elongation stepping from mass.

The rules routes go by they weakly expend from autotonic line, these spans include repeaters in short semijoin.

A line among shafts the premises of them unconverted, a law high with floristic parcel. Past virgin forest any secular rooting diminishes the rotator. That this induces a line-encoded antibody will sit secondary by as little, far tighter corridor straits than any sunlit above-ground percher.

What cannot falter a line's adoptional venting it here, the fallow of trees in arbitrary of consent to map, every late decision laid mat. The mapping lane won't sift what it strands, beached with no single existing reserve.

Band-stratified, they tender mass for map. By the shade of an attribute, it mulls a graph in fir needles. These pointer reducts strewn over a conformity with never an after all for the isolation. If likely to occur, mapped: subsistent in the identity uncover, especially *not* covered by any leavement existing. Merely to go to the front of our rows in the forego.

As though upon map such trees are never shed. The make-shade a heart per unit of rising stance compended, requested. Deriving what no habitat measured, but leaved among any linear description mapped as hid. The moss layer was marked into the directory of that reserve.

Lineage gratefully marred of little districts in a tide of sequence. Goading an industrial resurgence of forest, line-ampling, relaying at cramp the lower fastnesses.

The tiller of reoccupation is scarcely a length in itself, its steerage a space unstored in any current respect for donor lines. As though its presence no longer deplores likage without coincidence, locale knows itself plausible to the linear again, with a community come-heavy at the shaded right.

> some particle in path line the
> revolute receptacle appressed

Where there might be a complete pelting of trees, and the covering representations would dearly unmock 'equivalent cables' as more length than difference, for what is less than is rarely unnovel.

> natural lines don't render unique their variants

> were mapped to soothe the insultant
> a net-stance short common duct
> to tremble posture by character
> outspar posted to homebox

> stands of *offering* disturbance history

The transmural brush on the duct, a single human calculus has its pardon in a solitary need aside, to be placated if spun through such lineation: its tenure on the correctional spine of drift.

Leaves don't rake the trees from the field. Linear-discriminant, it is division's receipt put through single locus. Scarcely will a tree imply foundation orchard, though the faintest vein of them gives structural import to deeming the tunnels.

I take an ecological common range along a band spectrally unique, a fine-divided gird will I. If the terrain is linear it shall spiral its orders of neighbour. A hood tested to such exaction is in party, but strained of relatives.

A positional proffering of gallery length affording the niches its number: a self-thinning line pushes out the tide at a rate of similars for neighbourless muster.

The waver of being found *only* to cover, the rent of a history of finding-fallen, reclothed without retrieval.

    residual forest by adjacent clearcut
    in some shifts the lop is linear
    but extreme capped attenuant

No revision is solely tree-borne, but interminably covered, shuttered. Shady habitable derision. The forest stood under trees as a wedge beneath its braking, to avenue at thicket by resection. Incorporate a map image of the tree susceptible.

How mapping by trees is unsuited to parody the conventions of the remote: stick it far from fair. Dividing up prodigious disbarment from the nearmost canopy of the lay of line: remand of forest viability to a branch of unenviable way.

This sharp place, needling the line which desists from invention but not by place. By expectation merely, unstumbling what has pointed from surface to surface and printed it line for line.

Englazed alive in sticks, pricked for map-read, the combs shaded upon an alignment alone becalmed. Where trees cover with indicatives any ratio to cover, the overcome map they speculate.

Thickness deceased in absolute arms, the relive portion enpilgrims line in want of an onward bond where demarcation had frozen leanness. This snare gives no hurt to a company of line faring narrow when it goes unclassed to its attachments. Call a backspan diserased which the prime compliances (limb sows limb) will not use. They name this incidental to the persistence *they* stump. Bare in venture unless line send to cover direct, not a mauled nature-does.

No maps without swarms, the charms of light lance within profuse alliance. Binds are chines. Mile-hangers taken up by these very straps, the bounds hanging off time along avenues pitched for the nearness of the hour.

Timate replication fluting case-ends in the skirt of the woods by themes the hours don't invent in. Drawn on a green thread as to any other line of variance, as in no other bending to wraps of graph. The store of line not a forest plot made form but the fir gaps poled into time.

Isopath map, impounded for secondary foci, ribboning the forest fetched up against snow-glade, assenting a main tree component came within glare of realised niche.

Quail this demarcation, otherwise revocable, not as such uncoverable. Its remnants, if not fled, are overlong crossing our maps of linear wrangle.

Among unpatterned numbers the niche of precision members. The map's obligation to meet arousal, appropriated, where the place is searched so accountably defence. A forest of what latter fortification, how brashed with scores, this pristine town of time in wood!

Lyricised forest already the violation scan I have chastened if exception be line. The purer not just for skirting but reverting offence within the shelter-animus of us about nothing more, but not *among* nothing more.

We can only plead forests prefer to outlive their middles upto as many futures of their accosting. The latency of their linear survival threading the vanishment.

All this being to pinnings a measurable tremble, when line can't strip link in the event's divorce of link. Not logic but a plan-fabric of the unstowed.

Can we cable the trees onto such becoming transition-files, zones served truncation? Can they avenue the steady readings of encroachment? The line long ago inserted habit, unless tree has chucked the local smite of it now, braked on limits where cover accelerates

Postformal akinship tree-with-lid, the ruptive cuperative able. In recremental line.

Scarred shuts as a function of the time-feed. The trees' light strung above, forever line-slung, beckons the avoid under shifts of lid. So unlessened, any lean of angle with line in, no missing serries in this propped flinch at cover, the curb leaning into the goings.

If, in being given form, the *unestrangement* could cope with the rallying, but alas! for the leapt folly of such pursuant green avenues.

Unlikely to be more bush-line pursing at forest. Any boundary is map-detection immediately *under* tree-height, or mere laterals not playing lost for shelter, less misdirectable.

What forest prompted this genealogy, laid into us for owners of avenues whose every fuel to be spent on our peace these restive insinuators are? The scene of a line's fold. We are flocked in a whispering of externals, when the wholly unbroken must be readiness itself. A priory of trees. From gaps within, where there is nowhere well between, can you trees insulate our submission without us owingly aligning the mapping power we conceded *in* you?

That trees point *from* the lineage they keep unburied, supplantable long grounds of the planted apprise. They convoke a now of naturals which, punishingly, is ourselves unplanted though sunk into a setting of all of their sorts outside, in fits to line. Which is still the here of 'not then' striking us down in presence. A hustle to stake out, in their bodies.

For forest is not the rematerialisation of its road, a ghost of irony is in spirit in the woods: its intractable reduction to a bedrock extract not resenting us enough, as though we were unearthly squanderings already accounted for. Succour us today along lines whose sendings are no looser from moves in sprawl. A frame of renunciation is itself no counter-verdant.

The woods of some certain accessory ventures all well, the map slacker to its bereft ratio. On such a map the season leaves or unleaves fairly a ride at a time.

All forests are virgin to the field of reserve, and as intricate to the beat of the secondary, a contaminant yield of preserve. Festered hold done its refreshment watch for line.

The blunder is mooted amid foliage, an extension lip is withdrawn into a den ratted by trees. This wealthy penumbra holds our revisions in a batch of their escape to the boundless: here the binder can as well botch shade on a neuter's drift from line.

Deduced as the most linear of determinations along the interest aids of the 'havoc' of the whole. Only then can rods of sanctuary, the line-ailments, be taken out to the runs of refuge.

III

Attempt the soft woods at their tenant element, arising dump terri-
tory from the stem upward. The maps carry out per a throat of
ascendant shade. Of bracts not stateable but the pinnacles' clamour
it is, flinch with uproar precise.

The order spread vertical with pines for shelter, sharp cover indirec-
tion upwood, pikes of it where openness is the narrowest frank of it,
trade the arbiter out of horizontal generality.

Large props don't converge laterally on what sustenance may warn
but terminate in upright loss, meanwhile the less it led ascends.

    resprout after linear burial
    neat of where rising from

The tree defends to green spite, few go out seasoned among these
reserves torn. With the bar across retreat budged lateral below,
egress had fixed its shorn spindle above.

Rather effete line conditions used in the terminal saver environ-
ment, so aisles weave penalties on the thin-days of vertical. The
barrage beneath is nature unshown what cradles, not tilting, crane
the trees.

What a recognition lair brushes to earth leaf-height composes verti-
cal to such sweep-off, tempting horizontal tapering from any mere
alongness of true moves.

If specious open then serious *upon* what doesn't delve again to a cover of the rising standable. The litter of height will house the woods.

They sigh in vertical emprise, and breach, and nod, pent in the air of uncleared lift. Astutest ascent slapped at wire in the root, the theft askance of drew, up poles fled parallels of any maze of line.

The angle is not a tree's supply. It plots vertical to press what the vehicle does not move, from your reticence of strafed concealment in this countryside of masts dipped rigid, vertically pliant. Surrogate surfaces inclined to gamble for their up-pin election beyond trap and adhesive forelimb.

Tie the calmative in high sprit, the green tower of this vessel selects upward from its opposition tray, there armours collect. The chancel of the disparagement leaps from erroneous arch. An overwed buttress clan when called upon to perform (worm) a colonnade.

The planet of this action is shelter-vertical, the plumule taken for a rota of sky, but not present above weaken. Secure-devoidant, tipplenty at tip's web-empty. Discontinuous as mayn't reforest *above*, but does the line's fineal shedding as won't deceive of summit. Clear to the only postviolence we have.

Then the tread on furnishable inducements of law, laddering the span of infill by their own upbraidable allow. Solitude bodes the venerable in tall juries of their attire. A discarded crest of the catchment of aspire, unsagging lateral rules 'for free', ghosting it home. Up a lean realm to rival bounty of the beckoned.

The future leaches out from pine-peaks long past, the tarnishing an upward attitude without hurry. For so long they told at top-point. As though symmetrical groups were the ill trees intend above. Crown the paucity of shade, hoist the prolific retinue of the made!

Membrane bound, increments of unfelled might still require a top-wood, its multi-arm for star textures, tracking deformable filament: the increase *not* linear with discharging elevation.

The forest refused to uncondition that much of its uplike towards dysfunction. It bundles the topfoils toward nurture, begs the stasis some tall port among them: opportune as any tangle misled to a subject's set-up.

The gathering a rehung on behalf of its vertical props which aerates whatever shelter may not divide from nurture as repletion, compulsion. A partisan climb where they arrear catchment at sources. In time to the one step from below any steep bestows, its slanting lateral in tallcase.

Nurture burses in extremity, spirally crowded, what the forest streams by climb, not for any intensity's seed of outline, is vertical for this extra-polar sake: to sew up erosion with suitable crops of the reopening but along a common spire, not the space, of the turn.

'the mute closure of foliage': the open tip of the vertical fined on narrowness by a proving lateral below.

Hatching the earth at the face of its devastation, in differential sere, the vertical soil. At a profile tip each soil mound or monolith was touched for tomb.

The only spearing a line distends is that between stem and shoot, the stock and the slip to height. What trapped elongations entire trees in their vertical storms pull back to following particles equally unstripped of ascent!

We are delved in the disclot of time but enplumed in a nonexposure so parted, so passing shade to height. No portent other than this mark sawn off, the blatant severing of base from its vertical fetch. The weathering of stitch in notch climbs on. So much blunted wood where the mere stacking of its verticals would be dereliction.

Can we be admitted to the nape of the finite? At a height of no generals for stop, but slighter and tenderest with top? The trees' recrest is a shudder rising off fortune allayable, the finishable infinite seems infinitesimal simply going by gain of modesty to modesty all the lengthenings of exhausted local peak.

We do not disentrap the earth since, but must loft our hollow (sprung cone) where the coverts are *not* skyless between shelter and victim.

A vertical reserve which masses its blown attenuation, the ascent leaps penetration in a brush with shelterable arc, wherever encroachment eschews tentaculars.

adverse to stem mixture, echo across
careful ration for inordinate commons
upward, picket the allowance of contour

What pointing feature of imposition will show where beech loses ground? The ratio won't be ceded by flatter reverberations of shelter, such avid belts were only docked in the ravage grown upward. What is spearing when forespent, what encoppices in vertical diversion?

Cotter the unstable in such soars above equilibria! Where tallness likes to cap-operate whatever has risen from its table, let arc as if ungiven, so upright, terminate in a rigid accent. Spiny quotas are limitable-infinite.

To arrive at the peak's ragged proportionality, appears grown to a non-linear, the finite infinite having the unlimits of stop be topped for: not an aberration in the disappearance but a regularity in the undetection.

It isn't shortage which is progressive to forest but a pinnacle sortal of none too alleviate a vertical, reboisement only at the rake through it of void imposed by the limiting envelope, the gap bestowed, hung to apex. Or no effective volume *of* vertical because there are discrete voids among the leap.

At mast a setting out (hived), in the cyst of a nuance, most uninfused in spires: the shafts, though, in easy rehearsal between trees.

Forestial duel, the familiar not bowed but fished above drop by an unfighting sky, then forced to catch at shame of woundlessness. A mature light-chafer risen to mere intruder-border. The masture swaps few lateral revisings off the detainments.

Delicate in web each forest-unlike tip, vertical elation, through what coils offended in length does nurture cast up these peaks? The niche-limbs steeple domus for whatever sky its infestation disposed. If you stay luminous a long trans-echo, you top out darkly at transcendent past-pathness.

The fir flanks, an alluvion along skies, a deposit not shaken open but its own upward fineal in steep silt. Not to be added to, a greeter the non-reacher by direction.

The map, formerly spread over find, troubles its rise from ground in needled sites only, printedly topophrastic. The floor kept dry from peristaltic crave haunts relief from colonising the scalar increase. The upcease itself was any climb in intimacy.

An abbreviant simmering, by lateral trial the eruption wasn't empty of staff. Let vertical strokes denude a much greater steerer into deploying stasis aboard pole for guide.

On stilt of shade this avid lift retires dominance itself, vertical sped how sold on line its lease from use! A cover which guides the dividing between holding and not owning, with the having as given no further under than: what for trees is above.

How a vegetable law in the ascendant will deprive any rule mobility of its *prior* freedom from cover. However tall the shade its hatching is neater in hiding than deeper to line, vertical aspect the most pressing *local* way.

From the timid estrangement we are dedicate to the shafting's unoriginals. Upon this species we are also *below* what pinnacle may be the offer of us.

A clear mast-line but stammering over a root-path cast clean to leading shoot: not being without provenance makes for indifferent continuation. Insist no emissivity needs correcting along phantom shot highs, lightly displenish it above.

The precinct of its non-emergence from the instruction: howsoever terminable, a line will indicate non-followers (shadow on line, not along it). Accept dragged up the back, to the transpersive roof of: infights of near-term consents. Where covert alone will accuse forest, tallmost lethal foliage.

Tree spires cowl in scares of limb, or the placehood whose spikes so unvalleyed the nearer horizontal hatched, thrown back naked into the bench of trees.

The trees lift hale with mergers of our intrusion, ascend to where tallness tends the empty wall. By this coping I can't rightly ease any exclusion astute in us, but don't hedge it either. Trees ache tall.

All of nature bored uncanny for the arisen hollowables: where tall is finish and vanished in spears unspent.

Verticality is neither betrayal nor extant before horizon. The most of such recess upstood to the tackle of its species. A low call from the tips of its pieces. Pinnacle-files split the up-apparents without felling the space, the sham of it but which never elbowed the unstitching. Hear stipulations of arduous remedy.

A crowded raft to summit, a pattern of end no fury when gradation hasn't preached on this platform of conforemost but ungapped betweens below.

The vertical atones, succinct, as it converts to zero but ramps the entire funnel of turbulence. Infected out mapping, a stint in its space where the climb to the unexplored is via fewer dimensions.

The forest doesn't have the use of human to its house, so cannot represent the native orders of its aura. Why is the waste comprehensive to such areas at once vastly reparable, but in no position to withstand the privation of ascent?

Though we use tree population as surrogate, the assertion holds for other quantities to the extent forest has been quit by pattern: any carrying capacity outrun by tallness, the serene stasis stretched to a point of intimacy above the neck of structural relapse.

The forests of the hills have burnt over the past, denudation offers recedures to a repeatable space, that it might behood the time singulars. The earth's skin too sensitive to touch unless trees prick first, and drastically pin thereafter, right through to sheltering it from rarity.

The habital guise appears most influenced by the single system 'stem' vertically loth but typed tall, shooting at death, the usual demise eternally specific about rise.

>no vertical clinging despite foraging
>for height, upright rest has
>sawn abuttals to relish
>dormant support length
>
>the regime inside the crown
>variegated, at an inter-
>ception of solar tradition
>
>penumbral inclination
>mimics assumption,
>discarded crescence
>the reachment of aspire

Granted a temple of lances as demonic text-sample, the moving arrears had raced us up the narrow outpost to fear the height of remnant. Cabling themselves to earth, the trees stem a mountain rather than extinguish poise, but daring to jostle the inroads of the branches. Only a figment of height stands out in the open than had stood up to cover. Masses of dry slash left for ground.

As if to restock the open with only a pension of its vastness, to keep in hiding a portion smothered of whole. Verticals are not particles but the updraw in sole quantity of pointed entreaty.

How openness in the code of shelter is tapered, the truth of feature *does* alter to the extent of a minimal concision above earth, as if to stab storey with the concluding build-up an earth is about.

Sheer into nature from spines extra, the fronds not celestial but set on end, beseech tip's end, to end here not at the set's end.

What *can* betoken the vertical if the columns entirely uncancel one another. Shafted an upward desertion which so many besettings destress: a cover whose sharp pillars won't bury the earth.

Postface in Paratext

Our approach to the lines and patterns made by trees grows encumbered from whichever direction we attempt to notice them, but by now we have thinned them to our fate. The forest, in these terms, doesn't solely attract suspicion as cultural alibi, a means of being elsewhere during the share-out of social guilt, but is a way of revoicing what comes to seem like an *innocent* origin for critique itself (lightening the burden by way of figuring a choice of where the burden alights on gift). Critique runs to waste a little in contemplating the terms on which it spends itself. The capacity for a degree of non-function is what it has in common with other wishful co-appearances, other inordinate priorities. Though not outside its own remand on political answerability, its partial shading out by forest makes common cause with that naturality in us which is less exemplary (though contaminated by all the provisos) than itself. An acquiescence by default which takes one origin in inevitable fault but which borrows another in the yet more public relief of common gift.

So I hope that the poetry offered here sounds like permission to speculate a way to the contemplative, as a fallow turn from/within the strategic. Poetry has never paid its own cultural costs in full. Significant art, in its phantom sufficiency, unassured of cultural efficacy by any other machinery, thrives on the actual offer it makes of nurture, the offer it actively derives, and must provoke a satisfied reader to fund the supplementary works of its defence. Art does not despise defence, and may (phantomly) situate itself as in need of it, but such an obligation doesn't itself materially constitute the invocation.

Given a linguistic condition which still reminds us of all the instruments we have, how much liberation from compromised familiars which crassly nurture us can we stand? What standing is there for that part of ourselves which has no imaginative equivalent for correcting nature, but where the cultural might be that capacity to admit to standing possible presences *minus* tools, a matter of relation that cannot claim revisionist adequacy. But the moment the relation is written the adequacy will be over-written to the point of contamination, will accuse contamination by trees. Yet the call for a concrete relation does not enmass an urban-theoretic thoroughfare. I will have to take the conservative position that symbolic impoverishment is real enough when it seems to underly a measure of innovation-hunger which pushes extremity towards the (uncuringly) different. If I believed in simple inverse agency I would say that the unsatisfactorily given (trees being less than fully acculturated) is just what innovation *per se* renders even scarcer (becoming a dark stimulus for what is already the contemplative rarity of trees). The exception which offers to take the next step may not be available in any way other than perpetual exception, or may be a purchase of unnecessary death from a necessary one, a revision too far. The poetry presented here hasn't altogether abandoned a language of regularity but makes do with a nostalgia of living beside norms of the living, not as a false starting point, but as the place where an origin is already to be found living out its contamination by the unpurged, or what in other terms might be seen as the grounds for sustainability. The point at which a language that so waits upon this nurture can no longer be pristine. *Predictability* may rake any figure that undertakes experiment in the name (a burden) of an admittance. The intention is not to extirpate all traces of a discourse of the same, but to take some cover (as measure) when a contemporary collision with a symbol-collecting discourse seems inevitable; when it comes to be recognised that only symbolization provokes a lightening of the burden from within invocation. This will have to do with (non-ordered) charged particles rather than with an over-reclaimed disorder of total discharge, the former not to be freed from a trace of rigidity which resists formulaic dispersion but whose recalcitrance remains figuratively active. Whatever we can adopt along these lines, however, seems already cast toward a language of exception. And the exception too easily backs into a feud of revision whose co-ordinates are less than contraries but still heavily mortgaged to notionally deregulated events of the ideal. A world of correct universal that reads *itself* as gravity unassuageable by gift. By contrast, the renewable opportunity offered by a contemplative turn within strategy's "always already" is more easily figured as the sport of a regularity, of a conformity: what it is that the associable is *with*, apparently by way of an asocial detour. This turn is become a classically weak desire, but desire for what in itself has no history of becoming any weaker: innocence does not cross horizons either but stalks us on this side of the mischance. Knowing itself to be one condition of the negotiation, to be diminished by it, but up to that point entirely what the negotiation had to be for. Poetry, by taking on so many identities of adequation, is never to be more than poetry. Poetry's self-chastening is also a borrowed hastening towards a *sustaining* reduction of all that more memorably now defeats it. It is not that trees lend us something back from death, but that they tender to us a little of that life which, as gift, proclaims a non-identity with the revisionary authority of death.

This is why poetry such as this invokes a minor freshness by way of expensive elaboration of speculative structures, the problematic itself read as a blocked cluster exerting a figurative repose between non-possibles. Impossible to unfigure donation, the reposition of the grant. Such a figure is most often a re-version in the service of reversion rather than revision: its only originality lies in finding new stages through which to traverse a not letting-go. More simply, the available language of *religio* today is one in which strategic vigilance is pre-applied, but one in which suspicion stimulates affirmation through a skewed generative excess as the path of a too innocently applied offence. The wrong which trees do at such a moment. The only ground of application there is likely to be. No form can recognise its implication in domination without also acknowledging that it extends towards an horizon of the given as such, though lacking any defence against a reduced economy of the "as such". But as space of wish it must head off too foreshortening a critical positivism. The speculative or problematic within such a poetic aims only at bringing about an opening move. It is a contingent opening rather than the over-implored domain of the 'open' as such. Through it all the familiars of compromise work their way out, or onto the field, but any asides of witness are less ironic than part of the curve of the speculative towards speculation's own non-exclusion from the contemplative. It is included, but its inclusion is counted as the differently-spent of itself: if there is to be excess of the strategic (which art itself elicits), some of it will overshoot to what can figure a contemplative gift known in the waste of the application.

Cover as fringe and cover as the side we are outside of remain invocable through a desire to negotiate with shelter, unoutraged by premature or ill-sited repose. Similarly, to meditate the alignment of trees places the language of cultural position and aposition at its point of commonest *dis*position, linear conducements too much aspired in social relief not to harbour their natural share of us. Finally, rather than seek to disfigure the hierarchical as implicated in the vertical, I propose a prayer of tallness, the upstanding of gift: that it may vouch lightly for those lateral dismemberments of us, not in the name of spiritual renewal alone, but as the intermittently common or stealthy ascent on the part of the lessened of us by far. A granular-vertical finite, cysts of the unsmooth spaces which constitute the finite's radiant shelter from itself. The apex of an invocation now a little illegible but still quietly licit.

Attached, Assoiled

(1997)

Prefatory Note

The poem speculatively commiserates a fatigue of forms, whose attachment entities have been forgotten or fretfully bestowed. Now, perhaps, we see the seamless insurrections of these sources, put to a mild disuse but still within the range of invocation. Their impurity, as dominants, opens them to correction, but also to an interim of nurture that is always besetting the world of origin.

The poem asks: how assoiled (*ie* soiled, absolved) is our numinous attachment to this planet whose only defence against what liberation makes out of indifference is to afford some ironies of local weight upon itself? This assoilment is the breadth of place absorbed in the service of attachment. A confinement in dust, but with an insufficiency to oust those connective possessions which can only be more than us by remaining tied to us: what we have (or what having there is of us) to bring to some conscientious appointment. Attachment at the sort of door more speculative for not opening, but waiting at a porch in what comes to meditate a partial stormlessness, the appendix to the house rather than the contentions of the house itself.

Whatever has the instinct of attachment operates as a careful fragment in our culture; the fragment's present form is penetrated (some time later than break-point) by the liability of not being a discard, but only gradually does it continue to own the vocation of an unsafe unity

The gift is ill-received as much as lost, and the former condition must go on figuring within a poetics of retention that would revise our habits of acceptance. Only out of this primal grasping can a poetic offering, along a road of self-forgiveness rather than negativity, be made. Without an acknowledgement of the charged nature of burden, of the fact that we are all owners of the fantasy of numinous attachment, alterity itself would be a figment. The unpossessed has translated itself into the unreleasable, but until a gesture is made in time with this burden, the resistance of the other cannot even appear. And if it does appear it will not appear alone, the power of resistance will no longer be confused with autonomy. The justified weaker term will have won a freedom, beyond strategic manipulations normalising opposition, to attach itself.

I

Beads of attachment weep from the centreless globes. Aggrieve in fixing-sweat pellets without coat sapped as thrown seed. Stray sets refer to be chidden. Are, in this respect of seepage, the distal of an attachment eye faithful whether anything unhideable wells out of disperse.

Wiped to crystals which precipitate co-section at friction, compensation is the brittle mud in aid of pendant crust. Nearby, from stalk, lack is resurgent, though seek it a moveable homeostock and put it in awkward worth of attachment-lock.

What at fastener is petition to a deadener staple pad: the filter ('expanded bed') only reacts in an attachment medium.

Where deformity was dominant by slip to protection, a fatigue in the consolate malediction.

When attachment makes composite opponent, a multi-abandon arbiter could cite plural pause pressing into the exception conjoined. At a low evacuum concentrate, over attached fully turbulent flow.

Axially shiftable, but using self-netting elements where some of the looted space is prevailed on to embolden a protective stripe.

A torn plurality which abides ward, approaching the rips compare to latch. A world crated in shells, servable less its fastening resonance. Idyllic attachment upon the ledges invalidates any correct asset of the disprison effect.

Extremely low misorientation wins precise leaning from compression, where integral wound is solemnly jointed, than ever threw together unpliably abroad, rigid for limitless: whose dispersal-seat sinters its cast.

Having which, capitally reserved unfocal, is not paid for in abandonment. We have not what to receive in renting out a former so minimal affordance, unoccupied attachment. Drawn, not voided, brandished upon what is not defected, admitted to navigating repair not what replenishes.

That notches into an attachment oasis whole sites reinstanced upon leave of release, that is, chosen to unvow stores by prerupt sacrifice. Restorer or bestower abound a cramming decease, then go neutral to a homaged excavation on the flat, mature-future ingravity. Do not, with any curing, contract to mourn through a prism of loosening, nor have it thought to pay off jointures. Those, which, on a geophilous dole earthed to barest open, we afforded not to have.

Unflourishing dell, do you condone, a ruin's lull you do go to, those of us who presume you for the wrong of possession, daring you no stems or stones for dejection of territory? Rebind us at a cumber no early cumulus of defusions. Become blame, stoppage is bedded with assignments, combing into whose shelter the accession was invited to be with us, not possessed of disposal. Become calm in a history of modest swooping at the gate: we never reown what it was had you unhook the chore of our attachment, saw you disconvened in fantasmic affordance not to let slip.

Recessed by emptied internment, it may not spend on us freedom from gravity in the intimate grain set in service as gratuity beset to grasp, held-being at a least exchangeable hold in having.

A counter-aspirant will strip to hasp let it untie, but is not enjoined the unknot.

Several in forum weaning attachment off its scale. The habitats, fraught in singular quittance, clash many-at-land one stage out from site, how it will part us from docile adjacency.

Journey to fade where sped, never seriously sturdy toward the unshed. The awe solely wrung from its spate belonging it banisters over us, goes with stepped inquest upon any drop in the liable-primal. Sooner be a convert to whichever surrender of ground is rift pinioning rage. Not, according to our set-down, any *stolen* companion of release.

Linked in flexed omission, a discontinued code is said not to adapt behind what never promoted to. The tether alone an astute at wrangle: to over-occupy conciliation at its reform of adherence. The deletion arm recurring even more snugly without steeping in the mission of its going.

Lean turbulence for a nurture harshly left out among the innovatory stifles, the prod of return-bud suborned upon the pyrrhic-pristine. A maltreaty in primal common attached at the cusps of any deference in severing-point. Flowering into vigilant tooth, accorded undecadent abstention among repaired venom.

Those constantly unstripped acceptations a merely natural consumer of its own contentions: interim collation via truncation to enlace the gutteral of our disposals.

Insistent banking into a husk no more pander-drastic than any other hoarding alive to a fallacy of admission. The burden numinous in its assumption of 'consumables by correction', prising up the overpaid ground with a divesting we mistake the poverty for. Whereas indigence is in the having.

An attractor enmazed to the heart, settles attachment tolling to pieces. Unmaking apportion in undetached apartnesses.

Local pullings by autohesion, inveigh a *convenio* pooling rules. The inobstinacy was always a-cling in us, yielding the dis-enfolding before a shallow fall, no all from hold. Let it hope for a sheltered attack.

No appeal to the waiver in given-being could itself covet renunciation. What we do not have is now again to offer a contaminate draft: no let-up from world glues. No surviving organic filler for world dues. Detracted terms without an endower in time of rancour: kiss the broadsmith of possessory separates. Impound the byway put out to storm, ripple in retort the cherish of unalarm.

Disattachment the sole finishable we *do* meet, nomadically a fresher insider prone to wander dead-end branches of the unravel: not the wither-other of attrition, but flung traces unbecoming the spare of ourselves.

High-spend allaying surfaces, with room into an opening of fore-hearth. The sill of a moveable catchment, affirms in simples a more inflictual confluence. Combined direct stretch initials a random. The globe shell spurns any frontal house. The pass centre of gravity doesn't coincide with its print of attachment.

There finitude isn't pure contingency but adequate powerlessness to disattach. Distress in treasure abides our one tie ahead of roam and resume.

II

The binder itself will report, by concession, to flesh's clingstone, though concussate by attached rejoinder: into an outranked baulk sallied upon earth. Self-attachment to cease with the allotment of fruiting-staves not quailed to bars, offended until entrusted.

The more ample a simple by accrescence, swollen hold will remit it store, but in reticence of grasp than in fruit set to fall. Attachment's bloom of hand-use a staple of the sole remission: the hearth when putting us by was equipped with every preliminary but this: no early apparatus in the ungrasped.

Willow, dole in grip of me,
compile me the pinch of wicker
if the releaseless is done
festering, do not pardon
me dominion in the unheld

Custodial bunching from puny analogue of disaster: an empaled marshall to admit the fitter attributes by disarray of our demeanment.

Entailed amends blow wrap
on bloom, hurdling out the healed
denials of effusion, no spring
of amplitude cares to desire ran-
sack by adherence, limply run
to yield a secular mould

off locular burrows of the wild
A path gone stale in the mask
has fruited on tactic of husk
Till attachment's vexed pittance
inhibit accumulation, well-
circumstanced to us
in high cellularity

Attachment's type in hollow proximity of feature, aberrances an instalment junior nature in their having. A measure below 'on active attachment' but enduring through all the weak senior homings of what could not be by visit.

An apprehensive beatitude over against befalling it attached. Fixed otherwise (by wise siege), throughout all appeals collusive-unasked. Or idyllic valve: only this conduit will allow such ease to examine the trouble's forsake, trample into a chamber of sedence.

Having is not validatory, but outlasting the warning in fear of fitter sequence. The union whose dative of overturn doesn't rescind what is thorn toward givenness befallen, unkeepings bleed *by* attachment.

If not a fastening element, then hastening prickle alleviates the thickness effect around effort of joint: attach at deepest spare area of dent.

To adhere despite unreadiness to occur, it pressed the world-leap to infest a condition of departure: retire any stuck gift's aborting it is not the datum of.

In that readiness attachment holds to the unsifted penance of disposable, getting it punished to possible, unpurified by innovation sore probable.

More fretful with incidence than abstinent, attachables finger the grafted stunt. Free normal mode with inertia relief. Root causes look from pleach-cut to a low-stripping technique: whatever defuses blemish of shelter fastened to underload.

Variant adjoin, in abject part union, acceptance's input a holoform particle winder. A parsed lingering off the chaff of contemplation's vagrancy. Brought to meditative supervision by a nascent leaf held less petitionary than vacant cyclical in a garden, or its quantum of cementive inquiry.

Green enveloping in dogged escapade against escape, continue trembling to be home of stepping surely through a slipped shut. Stay there in continuant space, where a sympathy cast its future on location by infraction, the defiant unreviser gone in strict forum of stow-against.

Auto-attach englader whose at rest has a contested margin of cease. Compression leaves the flood at zero growth minus mouth. The shallow core which poses dread around remainder. Apertures resettle copiously about her unstirring pore.

No rift from hance, huskless while at insupportive origin. But adherence to handfill at a lower sedimentary severity. Unconventional in trim but not uncovenantal neat.

The arrangment saddled well until attachment was bursed by incre-
ment. Persistence by mote overly diagenetic than when at reach of
portion. The meekest saving of eternal alteration across the sand of
evolvement.

Not the found anonymous subornment in its finals, but spiny
branding on a momentary compass, compression bent against an
oblique token of the unrealisable. Upon a shore whose acicular
combing is empalement to appease.

Powerless to repair the occupied, phantom in strap only in order its
radiant *in*oppressiveness might not dare outright. But continue
toward the impurities of attachment.

True dependencies misjoin here in a mix of what might be better
unwithdrawn. As though this miscibility gap could be the dissipa-
tive for annexing by, a discipline to circumvent the dross of attach-
ment, all the joining technologies being pitted against any real of
load. Yet a convolute of fastening problems *has* come, opens 'no
holes' toward the composition. A centred crossflow stationary to its
neighbours results all the earlier in local transition. That these
troubles might convey a dynamic of attachment: interbasin trans-
fer static.

III

Even at rest there was asymmetry in the baseline shoulder, 'settlement' attached by shadows of the mechanic stimuli, a past forage irates new sediment. A joined lip might communicate this expiry to in/out envelope, the coil accelerate towards an inhalant chamber otherwise sapped of resting potential: null effect of adherence on the other solids. Channels falter of sufficient slip, no abrading of trough through to baulk once they have abjured a cavity of adjoinment.

> Prone to insulation then un-
> vacant at buried green, recumb-
> ant field no swimmer for
> elevatory wane

> Native resting plateaux
> sparingly ajar at aggre-
> gate, rescatter to direct
> neighbourhood of the caution

Contamination of ground as not doing without: source puddles sift of source, compounds a burden-positive fluid held to a raillery of offering. The non-avoidance of meld we do scarily pestle home.

On uneclipsed siezure of impart, more porous than merely maldecocooned. A repose descends as in actual sequence stolid with presignation. Chastening, re-acreing, but glomerate.

Repossessions whose coating-injection replaces purchased choke. Attachment without devout implement, scarifies the cyst of my belonging, teases a paradise of reliance, own to a ground without demission.

A this-way's adjourned park, paradise caged over a whole earth's dispannier: why are we not original to disperse it? What called to by the assigned which has? Vying for its hold from ill between us, we enlist a carrier to behave well to began.

Paradise in purse over the whole communicant worth why we do not smile awry its one-another, with spoiled attachment-set to abstain us. That the thickest cover of it won't keep our night? Tarnished to solutions of enfoldment in full daylight.

Viable in a knot of air frayed to centre and uniset as fledged from fresh at edge. An invigilant habit stun-visited or a seed dodged from hurried hurts, curt lodging of us so girt we may not overrun.

Stragglers of separation from behind content (in kind) is a solitude of veneration abiding its over-enrichment by attributes considered owners: whose arrear to commend is: stagnant, the vacant mobility is also a falling behind.

Conspicuous linking, whoever lids the web: quilt for quit on bolted stealth, you don't know the hearth of the bit. Where roots wrap thorn in incautious store, bold bed without smart, a prick away from adherence.

Multiples the insistence gravitates to habitation in hitches of reliance. The inclusion a lenient coagular stop at else. The incursion revives a stasis clean through redoubt, the resolute of strange storage, an involute of prevention at moorage.

Accrual in a fallow insularity of consent: how it attaches without ownership, but relies on a restitutional memory as ligature for free. Assumptive pandering of locus enjoyed in packet, not by exclamation of preserve: but the reclamation's fee it was sponsored to squander.

Increments of the refit trapping at world's inadvantage, the clements roll into folds of baulked pledge, celebratory in element: according it what is its non-empty weariness.

Which seems a ploy of the eliminatory taken in a consoler play of blank retention: a fragment of means quoting locus to attachment in onus, the refruits become the separability of its inclusions.

Not to flee inequity calming the domain, a reclusive exaction at the gallery of scree whose disclosures enter the vale of its insistences. Habitable earth, as if it were not crippled by rind, adore poor geoadhesive.

Rank recession into its far rest-stance. For all an earth is processionally winter within that hobble of fruitfulness on hold, on green grip to anchored deadstick, stripped to the bare state of it lasting. Rare knuckles of attachment in bud.

Where the preliminary flakes get grazed, coating so loath to retain though the contact denigrates, in poorer wetting to the separation haze. Sluggish to speculate a secretion until banished to protective action.

Rest-riven, adopted from its source-docility at brisk repositories, grief-amain in serves of wild. The social regulars of rest, upon fair emotion formal to the ration of repose, attach a bare lassitude to the interweave.

A stronger rest-taint than rumoured by snatch, amplified with no seemly nearing, no slow unattachable contrition. The intersperse of occupied distance a fate of repose. Tied to an edenic belt, storms trying for the tie. Crust crewed like squads run upon hampered strait.

Abraded like the interminal it is but which braves link, certain brevity to be unabsorbed over and above remaining. A blister to the replenishment across its long tacit revertings.

Fractured belongings without insurrection to depart, this non-comrade doesn't convert simply to attachment but to scarcity in its fructure. Bound up in natural lack which doesn't assert itself as a spurn of desire, but offers itself to whatever the naturality has already taken to itself *from* desire: that sounding between fluid spine and cornered tissue.

Based on a hybrid recess. Attach shielding to the backshell of work-surface drift. Survival as the outer monolayer, inaffordance of expanse in crevice-release the next outer.

Keys to global surface strand support between this virginal acceler-
ator and her own irreversibly implanted urban wear-plate. Securely
attach the body arid insert, to proximity of sown flaw found.

IV

A sign-strap which supplants the standard, or what goes stem-afloat in it drawn among the stranded. Attachment by debt-of, the field querk of nil change. Essential arcady in the much reduced concentrations knowable by adherence, to become it due poor paradise, no fore-tie arising at incumbent migration.

Insistent fold this far home can only mind the seclusiveness out of far other compress of regard, a disfilled quiet splenial in provision.

Dead detaining of a non-fugitive that has copiously strayed behind the figurative. But any 'lapse outward' resembles a lake for the measure of it, no more breached upon totality than the consent of it is pierced if it would not be perched. Auto-agglutination detained changeable, the transitive hold unmotile.

The cancel around attachment-to behaves sparingly by obtruding as much of it as is unowned into the given-behalf. We don't ferret predominance home-prone from the unprovided, it elides no given-at-made. Unevenly forged, the ownership of it is serial release, into the unever of the binding.

Expositionally traded off the ungiven of us, what cauf of whittled grass there is in harness! A soil scalds assuringly in young or old sills of the *below*-proneness. And would defect to the rehumation if it could be adulant shorn, shown given.

Where an aporetic non-possible is going to be left out itself, if not for the accomplished impossible of *dis*burden: so it falls that the mediation has no virtual dissemination outside of the assignment's being pipped at gift. The scatter can only borrow a heavy affordance.

This is idyllic valve not seated in contritional velvet: any further-than-given from which the ungranted of us steepens is surfaced to a penetrant insufficiency which abides the given-in-sought. Attached *at* the severally betaken, plural in accompaniment and inseparable in cost, not retired in origin only to scatter *from*. Horrendously fledged what is thereafter unfled.

May the gift assuage what is goodness of fit were gift given up. How is it unexchangeable tide makes mild connection alternating gift with the nil return of givens? In the neap of attachment become sparer reserve, in the ground of least swell no fit offering by abandonment.

Unparted incidence, infra-duced, stanch-stepped fiduciary hurts of the holder. The enormous end-climb pencilled by title to incline, does but tile over the slope of it stretched in stance.

An adherence donating attrition, lean forward the offer dour for us. Tuition of the gift researches out of entitlement but avers disputable hold, set to strike a long way down the unreleasable. Where it gives fruition is bite of a sourced non-fission.

A being-given will be harrassing its own fund, consequently abhors no nook, grown down to. Binds itself to the evens of any assailable riven, not refusing the local analogy of enchainment.

To over-occupy conciliation at its let-go to adherence, acquittal's after-effort given a blunted circuitry. Their scenery of dispensation: a languidly aloud factual will by all sizes seek to ungrade the hook, confirm without siezure what it took

But restitution has to be assigned, it won't well up in refreshment unless ringed in retraction: the touch of it rebought us but caught substance at a subsistence: by tenter-hook suspends its slake on any venal by-product.

Where infusion circumvents itself in retirement become sinuous toward the contained. Mystery an associate precedent not counter-distinct but remotely attached: a district divided by loser area doesn't undo remaining full by taint, tenement in unowned deliverance.

Until estuaries of the unseclusion become the familiar lenient coagular: tandem at hearth-side, how what reposes survives the outcross of locus, contrives not to repeat any other surpassing, the inswept it knows too much of.

Inanimate to attachment, stigma of the globe's fallow local. The gradient stammer which haggles to an unfinished of the wholly open, as, if given, not wholly open, poorer than fully bereft. The attachment knows of many hoops that jumped masses.

Clamming in the deponent zone, not restructuring but as if by a sudden loss of restriction flooding the array's outfed daughter-board. Diversity is what attaches.

Whose savings defensively associate with a discharge of equilibrium: attendant on the insular storm of a riven system. Spoil 'normal' relocates the assoilment to a hybrid thrive-line become native toil. A versatility 'that each one pent' given most recoil from the flawed dispersions, resemblance sworn back to figure by asystolic concession in the lending-house of attachment.

October 1994–April 1995

Parallels Plantations Apart

(1998)

A beam slants between the fir-trees, and particles rise and fall within, and cross it while the air each side seems void.

I feel that there are infinities to be known, but they are hidden by a leaf.
                                                                    R. JEFFERIES

I pray God for trees enough in the posterities!
                                                                    C. SMART

Ring, for the scant salvation!
                                                                    E. DICKINSON

from the ragged prose clump

            unarmored amid
glued piecework
                                                                    B. GUEST

solo minimamente sopra il suolo
dell'impossibile
                                                                    A. ZANZOTTO

Preface

Plantations not woods, given that not very much wildwood survives in this country. Why plantations for the purposes of poetry? They encourage a swerve from the forest of the avant-garde, towards something more like the cares of an encumbered yet conscientous settlement—or rather emplacement, however unsettled may be the chafing and condensing of bounds. It is a policy of marked-earth, an imposition which still retains an opportunity of becoming more slight, more self-attentive by such means. A plantation is not a garden feature, but a naturalised outdoor resource, perhaps ready to become a constructed confider of sources, a delegate (from primal forest) impoverished enough to refer to the human appetite for shelter.

This writing attempts a study of greened enclosures, manufactured as grids or reserves. It counters a world in which the purely open has for too long been compromised, stimulated, by urban expansionism and by the denatured figure of radical desert.[1] As a sort of postmodern greentown, on the other hand, plantations also belong to the urban series, but may be on the way to instilling a renewable shade, may teach us again the stickiness of fragments of reserve, those intermittent micro-bombardments combining as 'repertoires' of local cover.[2] So there is a need to desynonymize 'shelter' and 'home': our shelter is where we do not live, physically or culturally, but where we come to desire our terrestrial dependence to be both a natural continuity and a non-natural sense of concern.[3] That sense of dependency, a sort of gift to ourselves in order to limit the otherwise unalive and costly scope of our own autonomy, is mediated (so often now) through patterns of dominance and environmental oppression. But by such means (which have scarce ends) we trace the patterns of holdings upon earth we still aspire to as the things which cover us.

The fraying between the natural distribution of an ecological network and a plantation's psychic charge (as a saturated object) is basic to my poem.[4] Naturalisation involves a transformation from nature, but in terms of a site so overdetermined that what intervenes in it cannot be prevented from dedicating some part of its secondariness to nature. It is what companions nature for us, and needfully and symbolically disinvents nature from the sum of our transformings of it.[5] It is art's traditional task of purification without legislation. Though we see into the relation and admire the turn of the secondary from revision to rededication, we don't stand at the point of that relation: we can only occupy an aside from the heavy, living plantational inscription we have, for other reasons, inserted there.

Despite my strategic reduction of forest to plantation, how much of this remains a reminiscent Heideggerianism? Heidegger's genius was such that almost any meditative language one wishes to call on finds itself largely local to the haunts of his philosophic turn. Rather than oppose a language of meditation to that of technological enframing, I attempt a meditative negotiation *with* the enframings of technology, to investigate what speculative skill in configurations can still avail us, as we draw toward the reserves of place *beside* the grids of site. The finitude I evoke here is not one 'thrown' upon temporality, but is more like a contusion of fates emerging from our (supposedly detached) crash onto a no longer recognisable natural world: one which as nest, fixture, cavern or roof enacts for us the very embrasure carved out and resealed by that impact.[6] The insufficiency of relations which figures blind dependence as a 'crash' also allows the natural to realign itself from within a world whose constituents do not meet (or fret) any the less, but where such meeting signs us toward both a voluntary and an involuntary self-lessening. This is nature not so much in terms of technology's standing-reserve as a compacted and raked-over preserve, and one which, despite the industrial handling, makes its returns magical and unprogressive.[7] Here may emerge the connection between plenitude and a persisting sense of natural insufficiency, as well as that radiance or *filled* boundary depicted as lying between the two.[8]

What do I mean by 'insufficiency', a term coursing through many registers in the poetry which follows? The crash back into attachment already referred to, a transfigured fixation, or fixity once more allowed to figure, can only be valid if it reveals an insufficiency, not of but at the origin: an origin which has after all been provident in its place, a plenitude reserved and interned in the scarcities we handle, and so not to be turned out to the counter-scintillations of a beckoning absence. The one element absence cannot overtake is scarcity. Don't think of insufficiency as less than the human, but as the lesser of ourselves (our dependence on an unsought life) with which we need to sue for relation. We can find in trees an externality whose ways are like ourselves, but which won't exclude us in the way in which we exclude ourselves.[9] On the contrary, insufficiency is recognition of what has been commonly *included*. If there persists an insufficiency of nurturing power available to the human person, it seems to illuminate a given reserve of the world which we agree to cherish. An insufficiency, then, not apart from an essential radiance; or the implementation (here figured as arbitrary closure or premature arrest) of a plenitude fully offered to the slightness of what can ever hope to possess it.[10] Where rarity thinned to an ubiquitous radiance has no contrast, no opposition: the plenitude is all the likeness of its insufficient occurring— hence the importance of analogy for my poetic.[11] Insufficiency is non-negative difference: scarcity's sleight-of-hand, however ontologically devious, is for us, I want to imagine, a moment of loyalty.

What is common to both nature and culture is something like a residual mingling of supplement and impedance, of universal boundary with (or within) local flow. This is a 'finite infinity' which remains reservable and so renewable rather than the 'infinite finitude' which peremptorily expels itself towards death, impatient with the very insufficiency which radiates between itself and death. It is scarcity, not predominance, which can defend itself (and vivify figures of defence) against any pure openness to the fatality of a narrowly temporal reabsorption, a fatality that prefers overmuch the *dynamic* of distance rather than the static and so less predictable lyings-by of distance. Material radiance isn't a transparency, but a glow weathering the limit and frosting the glass of mortality, bracing it rather than merely breaking it in the *manner* of mortality.[12] A gift so tremulously given does give us the space in which to resource the findings by which to accept it.

A word on the names of the plantations themselves. *Dur Hill* is a modern inclosure in the New Forest, planted, if my memory is correct, in the late fifties or early sixties. I remember struggling over, as a boy, the deep furrows which had carved up that part of the heath prior to planting. Even now I still more spontaneously visualise the area as open before the trees came, so have picked up the invasiveness of cover and its deep underscorings at first hand. I never entered *Throwley* plantation, only having glimpsed its packed rectangle (of what looked like larch) rising up a flank of the Manifold valley without any hope of covering it. Though small it is equally careless of the contours of the land, so that its short brushwood takes a firm venture towards not quite open horizon. *Duke's Plantation* (on the north-eastern foothills of the Quantocks) is a nineteenth century stand of beech and oak with some later spruce and larch. It trespasses up the former 'smooth . . . airy ridge' above Nether Stowey known to Wordsworth and Coleridge. The poem ends with another small rectangle of wood in north Cotswold, near Blockley, a favourite haunt of mine for some years though I didn't learn its name until I came to plan these texts, by which time I had already assigned it to the close. It juts into a small dingle with a superb long, low hanger opposite and is bisected by the footpath which goes across. Not more than forty years or so old, it is named *Central Wood* on the map, though I have since come across a name-board among the trees themselves (mixed beech, larch and spruce) which simply gives it as 'Centrals'. So, of course, I have allowed this rather linear and unnucleated site to provoke another negotiation between the dynamics of place and the disposition of a centre. Here the 'centre' seems to emerge as a nub where an excess of concretion turns instrumental, or especially fragile at its reduction to hierarchical guardian, but still willing to offer extensional cues from its own indurated self-placing. Its stasis can be troped as a fallen coagulate fragment of sustenance: some chastening must be possible of our own accelerative consumption of pure disjunctive creativity. I don't deny decreation a role (what moves could I make without it?), but it tends to dabble too much in a general non-satisfaction of relations rather than a generative insufficiency. However, the strewn necessities of place still call for a tartness more prone to affirmation, or for a severity which lessens itself enough to make the terms of inclusion appear where we cannot usefully oppose them. It is much more productive to consider why they have, just here, come to impose on us. If a centre is not the key to the whole, it is nonetheless a break from any seamless network of interaction, painstakingly reverting instead to a moment's hierarchy both arbitrary and sheltering. It is shelter which remains open to the visitant because its complexity is no longer of a purely ecological order; rather, it has assumed a contrariety which holds it in a spirited place, hollowing out the waiting arena, not from a loose open fabric, but from a knotty excess of the offered and covered burden of centre.[13] A counter-friction of reserve centred beyond the speculative fabric of relations. There is always a dysfunctional residue in the take-up of nurture. Is this a scarcity too much desired, too prolifically resorted to? The centre is a figure of arrested network overlaid, usurped by its sacral standing, but always admitting the light of insufficiency to the loved relata. Will this explain how plantations mainly linear have now come to be what outposts we have of concentric shade?

Notes

1. The desert as a privileged terrain of dissemination lacks not just sustainability, but more exactly, frugality. It is frugality we entrust to negotiate between ourselves and our attachments—and only to frugality could be confided so fraught but essential a relation.

2. For the role of 'repertoires' of cells of variant stickiness within (or across) organ genesis, see Karl Kroeber, *Ecological Literary Criticism* (1994), pp. 143–48.

3. Culture may indeed be the human real, but not be the appropriate scope of human concern-for.

4. See Jean-Luc Marion, 'The Saturated Phenomenon', *Philosophy Today*, 40, 1/4 (1996), 112–23.

5. I am thinking here of the need to avoid too subversively smooth a blurring of human/natural relations, or of what has already been called 'humanature' (see Peter Goin, *Humanature* [Austin, 1996]). An active disinvention of such a compromising natural both reinvents the nature of human intervention, and tries to promote a space for the natural to remain, not unknowable or untouched, but *relationally companionable* by remaining dimensionally other, though not absolutely different. The symbolic process, as I invoke it here, where it loans its difference to the co-presence of the other (simultaneously less-than-other), also affirms the prevailing scarcity under which and as which a material world attains to its horizon of plenitude: a consummation only presented to the scarcity which evokes it, and which is affirmed (affermed) as scarcity by such co-presence.

6. For an earlier poetic exploration of the embrasure in terms of a sink, see *Seek Source Bid Sink* (1995) in this volume.

7. A technologized landscape dramatically enables us in one direction (and has its own internal, phantasmic values), while disembodying us in another—an economy too easily confused with multi-dimensionality. Can a thick materiality (our contemporary fabric) ever re-embed us, or is it more a nomadic lava, loosening old, retentive but thinly tree-like pinnacles? I don't think it can unless a more creaturely deference on our part attaches this autonomous materiality to an horizon simpler than its own functionalities. Simpler than (and so more radiant), but not freer or more innocent than: there is no re-attachment without contamination, without symbolic predation.

8. The idea of a space of separation as a filled difference comes from Luce Irigaray. See *The Irigaray Reader*, ed. Margaret Whitford (1991), pp. 165–67.

9. Self-refusal in the name of difference should not lamely amount to a refusal of the non-different other-self.

10. The given, as apprehended from within thoroughly compromised materials, resists blockage, but once the given is acknowledged, it stands itself in need of figures of protection, and re-introduces a negotiation with blockage. Blockage not as the ego's refusal of growth and limits to growth, but as the

tangible cumulus/detritrus of commemoration. The radiance I invoke is itself headed off *by* insufficiency from a tendency to displace the given, and remains open to an assignment of grant, the openness here not being any simple lack of ligature.

11. I agree with Michel Deguy (*passim*) that it is the possibility of resemblance, not difference, which remains the more surprising: a matter of holding an object at a distance but acceding to its semblance, living the alike through an impossible fidelity. I have also been excited by John Milbank's treatment of analogy in his *Theology and Social Theory* (1990), pp. 302–06.

12. The concern is with what nurtures rather than with what intensifies, to avoid pursuing an accentuation of the materials of life no longer on behalf of life. This latter path would be to envy death and seek a direct appropriation of its sublimity, rather than filtering off that milder radiance which only the scarce of the living can siphon back from death. Such an apt donation foreshortens life but does not pre-end or proleptically terminate it. Death within scarcity is then sufficiently present for the determinations of mortality, realised as part of the temporality of the gift, but not contractually returned to as a being-toward-death.

13. This thread is pursued further in my essay 'Tutelary Visitations' in Paul Hills (ed), *David Jones, Artist and Poet* (1997), pp. 141–157.

I: Dur Hill

No longer forward of us, but extra grant in the complexion of terms, the clausulae of winnowed degrees. The tree a slight increase into the manner of defeasibility due woven feature: as block of green, forever switched through, sprained of recovery.

Heartland stiffen district, the impingement will expose a tidal green, unrifted how indurate, a slow surf driven onto conferral. A carton of woodland dumbly open beneath the arrival pelt of trees. Control which has tossed its grain to the rare fibre of ground retempers that particle, deserves with raptive ventricle.

Precedence in a slender case of woods to abridge feral re-acquaintance. Where trees have shot ahead, before earth abrades upon itself.

Something magazined by standup of forest, but now with a plantation's burden of startup, imposed before any grant to position had truly appointed reserve: a thing of resource merely a course of insufficient feet bearing into seed the treadlines of earth.

Indemnify its recalcitrance, mark the pro-widening gyre shorn of outcome except its own concentric flux of reserve: what would be bower in zone has broken to shelter among the lance-guys of recessional community: rope natural climax come ashore beached on organic duds of tree in niche.

A brace not apprised of liberal lodging, with no skill to dispirit the underbearing, until some ill adoption houses an adept in grip of the favour towards radiance. Without natural copy kept within earnest of spoil.

Notifiability of shelter ahead of its surround, the lyric open is latched from distance: sunhaze bushed clear of opaque brushwood at a translatable encasement, its erosionful universal.

A wrong of speciality cherished among reverting narrows of growth-point, ostentation to requite seed here where the error settles to vocation, freely infests its truck with earth. The penalty of incursion it will not commonly desert.

Robe in rote from plantation's initial stasis: see the grower foiled in a reflex flower-of-leaf, become a giving thief from the mono-sower.

To embellish the circumscription ravishment is stripped in remaining incomplete, hidden from end by unachievement. But where insufficiency has emboldened itself radiant to ends: finitude, asymmetric in offering, here subtracts the equality of a middle death. Completion might then haunt a shaft of wood for the relay-sufferance, offer its overshot origin a collection-path: assigning the four non-comers of horizon, where the leap of birth is out of view, to this hatched allaying of radiance, observed in unadditional light.

Not a welling but a ramistitch, in repair of a culling, a unit which begins again the attentive insufficiency, housing less of the innocent finite's accomplice than companionable gleaning from a reproved field of assistance.

Co-trussed, but seeks in demonstrable stead that compression at touch-light, bud-tight appartment: like a chrysmal failure shining itself upon a shadowable entered sun from behind each sash of forest.

Abjuring convention's unlock to renew a more primal reception's disseverable stock. Fruition about a burden of unplenty, radiant to the place enclaving without installing.

> Mean stand volume, strides to stand.
> Solo biomass above ground.
>
> Threshold by radiant pale, adjutant
> saturation survivable by insufficiency.
> Riser rather than receiver.
> Repose a holder of non-returns.

Vastness muttered with thorn, now made moderate to accommodation. The invisible world has only this visitable-shelterable for refuge, but when housed behaves unfairly as any token in this wise to have escaped from its need, from this mild espial dear to the wood's spaces of stop.

Untrapping itself from heavy befallens beating up from distance, nourishing a cluster across the wood's unison nearer by far: does this accommodate those organic changes in sapience not already communally redundant?

Both access and distance are plantable here, where they may not be, in this green grid, interwoven, intervened, what they otherwise are to each other.

Heavy fibres of world, not for so much longer will you press into vacuum as though independent of the interval grain in this wood. Cleansed to its skeletal but unnaked thread, while what was with you was cramped radiant without. Open the insufficient universal which all held allows out to.

Intimidating a thinness not caught on distance enough, bio-extant not at the serene limit's cramp, but its post-severe retreat before shelter, before shelter's name for the advance of it.

If original woods are waived, it's not with the consent of stems, not a relief from proliferation: the beams of return are bundled by the light's own order of return, unlabyrinthine-bright within leaves' omenta.

The brimming would admit that radiance as mere entourage, were it not for the plantation's own mal-attendance: if cloistral, hard to expend by, a harsh alliance justifies its unique to serve. Safe to preserve but reduced to nothing but its kernel stamp.

No banner of infraction, but hearing common descant with smother, bridling the tucked light, the rocking requite, of a freedom with the insufficiency: undiscardable stasis of the nemerose in stubborn guide before a more proficient finite.

Plantation of paged tenebrae, safe-site on the plateau's harvest narrowing, you are the rearmed space across which an uninhabited door has fallen. The door's function survives, or appeases, the house's useless copy-conversion, into a city of itself given that all doors multiply toward forest. Where door to forest, stripped of the forest's house, is plantation.

Latent pressing of the earth swung off the trapgates of the wood, unsteady in release as stilled from increase. It won't have protruded our before into our without except via a caravan of its own. Is this a nourishment citifying the opportunity to trespass? But where the limit goes hard with us, so that any wood-specialism is spent shelter-brilliant: it must subtract from us our radical which could hardly weather the re-intention of it so planted up in pulse. The exemption by which we are shed to it, a demission of ourselves we cannot put to it.

As a subversion recalls when quieted, its unsolitary bonding of depth on defect, procuration of planted norm. Immune where so applicative a sacrilege, what the trees fledge against seasons in flight.

This prising of an insufficiency out of the prism of ragged leaves, fitting the zigzag incorporeal thus miscreant, not quilt into it. All fretted leaf on the tut of its worked alive by sufficient isolation, treats condemnation to a green visor.

Even at Dur Hill a plantation, green with shell, embarked upon its sect, treads columns over a pact with ground it is confined not to choose. Treads-in a least lastingness, drilling the pound of pine-seed, within the pound of the least cast.

Flinging from grief a space abrupt in grains of residue, illicit prefer-
ment impounding theft. The old pollution from primal wood not
allaying its pulse. No earth as penetrant as massed tree is.

A radiance embedded within insufficiency must spring home the
regularity of it, be at angular trades: familiar to grasp a diminished
roof direct through the tools in trees. They prick a pinnacle of
repose through what in any other core is a mere grotto of stunted
light.

An included parsimony benched around excrescence, round any
season making ploy of the chances swapped for wrap: fold upon
fold of exchange empty for a content mustered, sourceful before
their burden absorbed.

A siege within port of chaptered forest, difference in brushwood
awakes to a stretch-haven. For no other woods is this small event,
naturalised by an unrecording scope preferring effort of shade over
written green feathering, so tasted by plantation in its fastness, in
the injured instruction we grow of it to recurrent warrant.

It seems the soul is so consulted, a hereof is amassed from the
insufficiency, radiant for the that of it, accorded degree, praying the
inequity of it: expensive offering deft for object, with what it isn't
efficient to contain, but in the way a finite never abstains.

As if amid this tackle of insisted growth there are purposals for a
lower number of forests. Whose non-harmonies press for a pleni-
tude of the empaled. Is fullness ever a dissonance? Who sieves
haven among her deflection spaces, detect to a smite in harmony.

Plantation without regenerate exaggeration, without considerate exile, the anti-housing in you is at the discretion of shelter: you don't forsake another's desert relief, their preferred irritant-inheritant as it mows the pristine, but you have still an uninhabited settlement of your own, culling the foreplace of opposition. You the insufficiency of what a displace always took, but grant no further revision to the secondary deceleration of it. Where expansion from eden grows indistinct, a stark park for any naturalism to steer: that redemption silhouette more of such hounded trees will not broaden. Until eden's expulsion foreshortens the generality, is plantation-bound in the woods.

By some soon-wanting fate, one of baiting the entanglement, too sudden, too close, too vast, where the insufficiency is set upright at stockaded planting time: which will nest in quandary a grafted given-onto devoting the organism of its reduct.

Very secure sectance: around the pure pine an horizon poor and apprenticed, on some universal scale not learnt for summation.

Or through it a straight wing fends off that huge nest but covers its decisions: the clapping shelter is feathery rather than reverberant. A thing peeled by lift grieves onto itself again, hooding rakes like apparel. Sifted to insufficiency, some due particles of surety. Sweep a pinch from the earth, between fingers of hollow tree.

Drop cities, so bed leaves. In plantation array what derives the covering reprieve is urban of shed origin, shade outside reserve of litter.

II: Throwley

Pungent in pine, snared candid across the remainder's uncovered hillside, a wood outside any majority.

Squatter with no furniture of the mobile, plant your hug diminished off salient, no huger unchange constantly thins this.

The stubby roost in mantle, where a slighted unnew pilots return, upon a hillside's recent luckless accordance.

This provinced central creep, secular steep, sacral speed come direct upon correct reduct, trees tipt to known zone for their crouchable: a mechanic of radiance spits local imposit.

Arid-mutant, but bought off attested barrier, as the better of small-change branch in tree-defiled area.

A satellite abroad from the inner famish, to where it furnishes ungovernable shade of the thinned-out: this the human clue launches up the hillside, towards a nakedness of stakes.

Perduration all swawthy espalier. What had detained an open from its parish-infinity will still presume on sapling, a subject scaled down to the seal of the world. Slits together at confinity.

That clear unripe face of remove never to grip beyond the moor's empty ridge. The varnished slope smooths deep under wind, the naked hill flush with this new static, where folded tree-table is tied to vertical twist.

A poll of the woods set opinionate, pine-lenten. Uncharging as winter leaf, the light too sessioned to spurn what a sky invites safe season windowed into, pennanted from below. Whether as blocked beneath, there dis-taunted.

A stubborn filter sets launched upon its standing toward the nails of place, fixity surviving as only half the shelter, but through edges fought over for an intimacy outsitting it: palpable instrument to crouch and retract horizon by the half of absorbable light which flies it by. The same half of shelter which flies and fixes to keep it half.

Tenuous pressing together. In a photo-herence slender returns on the openness of light: but unfelled radiance from this tender loss of result.

Only the trees admitted back to squares of kernel no longer rob us of horizon, reduced now to their swabs of replenishment.

Bony parapet at an untorrential hedge of themselves, takes refuge upon the usual unsurrounding of light.

Throbbing impediment turned alcove, a rota moulded on the pandered shelves of tree-level.

Then small forts, squarely, merely, browse on their danger, encombing a light of the hunches of defence. With hazy rotation, it scrutinises the needle deferences.

Insinuate selvage, cadaverous but with filter set selfish green. Some unemergent regularities, composure conning common proposal. Green hostility seduced to a perpetual clot in the wood, peck chain from holistic braid.

As though shelter can be done in team, unruined in ream: frequent brush with love acquainted with the lowering that honours salvation. Brushwood not naturalised to the passings of light, perfervid at its panel.

Squat tower of the green-grey trudge of regulars, bearing on the ridge, a proneness unburied but unwieldy nearing its marriage: links of shelter immoveably unfallen, is it that a stasis can rear no heavier impermanence? Gives root shelter to what is identical-*un*invented of a differently suffixed earth.

Insufficiency must be stasis freed to be no less patient than its own continuance up the planted hill: overtakes advance as its cladding does an unopenable readiness in the seed.

Production rushes a spectre of world to sector, the human order lacking spathe, slight-spiked shelter to speak redress in type, here ties itself to an agenda of the slots of resonance, aprovident set-aside. All the woods of it one plantation incarnate: stake the step between itself and plentifiable horizon, our solitary provided set-before.

In this placard of wood, fractionally granting thorn its tremble. A green sharpness of the never uncovered. The copse has ebbed into valid attrition, ragged dimness to a setting of defence.

Anchored to poke the gust toward sighable impasse, scatter glades from the pick, an axe-band of site. Petal-verdure in its mean of distributed order, one pine decipherable for a tranche of unfilled time along the spokes.

Infestant grapple, a cluster engreens a latter rake-out of earth in tree-habit, a bright horizon which can't be cut out of battening onto woods: in aura scopious of this over-sown dimension, untorpidly knit and shaven.

A wire-like stretch of simulant glade, the clamps fetch all that won't forsake a real of trees by plantation. These green racks are the fault which roots me to conjunction since, well across the open of any hollow joint in previous rock: the full cleft stands stone to first call, its repeat begs shelter's smarting knock.

Oppressive uncovering thrown to the pounce of reparation, the leap of the construct onto its awning: with cropped shins of harmony's arisen memory, the ounce of completion. Unicited green, the curing myriad uncitied.

A waning bower with no sense of end other than the plantation's stark contrary assart across ample, empty, sufficient hill. A slide of belonging planted; streamlined, to a standstill. That a dwarf share of thickest orchard will linger at the shade's stump. Green neon of a forest's aversion, was the city precursor so much ironed out as porch to the woods?

The row is content with brushwood with which to scour an earth alone with itself, the satellite of loss raised to invasive heights, requital upon boggy loft now observing green forbearance. These trees will be harvested without flush, detectable still in their interlude.

Mechanised forest for its contribution intensity, its blinding input, the spatial-cornered as world, but as idyll crannied and packed, unable to be sole picking of its industrial-forestial origin. Put purity through this cable and proliferate the convergent riddle, the divergent middle of bind.

Drawn in to conform to your unstricken, staked best: 'rows-in-case' confected by petallic, unmeandering earth. A drill sore sown to earth-cred, relapse in fringe thronging to full fallow circle.

Scantlings capable of carrying forward a net sum usable in world section. To swab a piece of nature, or make it peel its own resign.

The favour of a world consigned to a fabric of deserving, leaves fining a brace of shadows against shake-out. The unsawn clamp, small pictures shawl the clasp, having intended this shirking for a texture of remission. A glade smoothed to awake fewer hangings of exported site.

> Salt of the tree
> Populate from narrow feet
> Your gear upon an industry of air
> Emulgent not temperate
> A weather of rebuff prides the tree in peat

At one equipped fate the greenish unsought of the world: a whole plantation of it dissembling, the machine in tarnished leaf.

> Hasard woodland
> To have hired hard plantation
> Heard woodland cry of its green card

Fragile tallies are ram-shaded by greeny salt. Furnished with not being passed over, on the strictest violated term of the insufficiency.

III: Duke's Plantation

A light of scope envelops a skimping earth, default to leaf circum-scalar in law, irradiant, removal. Clothed sharpness in spruce, barer decompression of beech. The wood, shown universal nakedness as much an elsewhere, here lit to a trans-acre starved out of digression.

Enjoin the gentle plight of florescence on a wood's conduit: of such fast, long-lived features direct no leak of pleat to earth. Release it cheap under holly, leats of the empty sun-draw.

Sharp of finder where found: accredits, irradiates, insufficiency in the scored travel of itself, bestowals at descendent percent.

These radiances were ill-posed, but sliced the plantation exactly displeased or juxtaposed. Inband of a selective, sectant scene, its platform jitter. Size-of-source the forest of effect at original bridge-magic, a finder found glows like posset of reciprocal symbol where common order curdles transition: or what a plantation partitions as no crossing *through* light.

Radiance unnamed for preference beside its limb-darkening model, hardbody plume, shelter requite pittance: approvingly supplied from reference towards insufficiency. A cladding eccentricity throws light round itself, revolving its portion shadowing compli-ancy through the no-refusal of an unresourced centre.

Attic radical behind barrier systole: a stray upper radiant in option-null imparting. With light almost occluded in a weather of commis-sion, now have it bowing toward glow, boxing to flow.

Leaves quicken shadow but slatter it where they draw on the pegs of light to perform the insufficiency. What is no support illumines the loosener at base, whose invitation this is, albeit relaxed to an avarice of absorption: routine knowing upon terrestrial forematter, the illuminable.

Leaden with vertigo of an exfiltration, slurred light will expel itself to the aura outside sufficiency. There where an unrealisable has no exit surety, it forebodes the unreturned as pastoral stock: the plantation's palpable entirement it delegates a re-here.

Where venation rifles the ray, slotted like tray in, tray out, among level deliverances of leaf. The coolness burgeoning from so many unspared pores, talk tares of invading refreshment, leaf unsewn under leaf.

Irradiance lap reticent in near-rared spectrum.

Veins of direct shade by a trailer to sunlight: radiance intractably coupled to shape, to shape's shade over its contactual, basking no more than the unhidden shutter in each leaf-trail. Here it isn't light-to-surface reluctance but plantation limbs to be spectrally resolved. A clutter of light admits overture shocked solid. Shelter to stand alone in yield of compromise obtained from the source aperture, fident layering of attenuation.

Prolong basement swung above surface when the counter-caller will enditch these brittle bowers for its glow they antecede: with hardly a deputable lower band around light, this is the difficult transfer to plantation. Cherish the boding if to expect radiative loading.

The kernel of fire to purchase within a race to insufficiency, lean apparency given radiative portions: an instood separative shelter re-exiled to relations of light cordoning the glade they are seduced to.

Move the tiller of the woods from the ply of the path, yet a path inexorably follows this leaning stem: a token argument of planta-tion guides the keel of the wood. Across a serviced paradox of light, toward a sufficient insurrection in the index of supply: greenswell laded from solar sky.

A window out of sylvan mosaic, casework to the radiance ahead, blemished by what crouching cabinet acquits entrance behind: solace derives from impedance before guardians, unimpetuous corruption into solar pardon.

Leaf calibrates in the fluked bodies of its prism, united white per void, it didn't ache to illustrate forest's conspectre: woods of a pris-oned count of diffraction.

The slow cadence of unwood, at plantation edge it needs plait dole of finish, onward tie enmesh light unopposed to pole. An insufficient primary about its domestic fate, local dress of high-risk parting. To 'bestow termination' at a collection point itself terminal is to follow a surplus identity winding out the radiant reserve, the opacity which focuses light stranded luminous at the derivative of reception, radial spent communicant *via* the insufficiency.

Switched into respite, let treeshape once tempt construal of shade, towards a brokerage radiant in shorn convoy. A bulge in the brack-etting, living off light, wouldn't otherwise slake itself on umbrella monoculture, co-terminals green to shone-green of such stiff infinite opening. Sees some harsher whispered moat around a diamond of need: torrent apply circuit on a speck in gleam, gleam covet leaf. A well of masts is convergent pause on suction, ascending thinly its capillary torch.

Whose tops sparingly molest the shine, compel refir at the scale of a neighbourhood manacle, reticent barbarism of tree to tree pairing the disportion light fetters. Mat at ingesting cracks, this litany, 'attack-divide' 'attach-abbrade', craves every ride its corridor to knot surrogate repletion: a stem of fixture awakes light awarding lot.

Where an outside has outclimbed its heart, the plantation must dip to the very stage of light which fires fabric in aid, to put steeper admission yet at some quite linkless revisioning. With tall expense of apartness, inner gaps beam towards a radiant trenchancy of tran-sition certainly external: eternal reclusion does risk narrowing these avoidances, or where insufficiency appears ahead of union, there abutments of light enlip.

The pine pier athirst for flame in its evening cleft, tested to a dust of congregation. Of sunways which have baited the long pause with spars of an unbelieved, a factor racked of shelter.

Lead the light away, halter departure to a tree gaining crowd on exile astray. I also see that irresolute subtraction from sender, replanted, spurned, at centre. Know a plantation by what it does up to plurals, what brakes-in before any spoke multiplies *on* singular stickings: concourse of sun and altered sun, of shadow and defeated shade.

To apprise them in their valley where they have no access, where trees apply to what they don't hunger after, a density capable of throwing it rich under the inter-particle belts. On trial throughout a spine of reintroduction, the eclipse off presence spans the insufficiency, conspicuously spurred. This credence arouses summer blankness, but betokens some easier season crammed to a radiance's irregular off such riddance. Roped to the shown forms of light, clearing the tie by a closer norm.

Even a minimal porch of subjection will suffice these circuit traps, dropping to common light the wood's angled outflow, a sweetened but functionally direct exhaust: to boost to a universal sharp reserve, snared at the least swarm.

IV: Central Wood

At roost amid the poles' mild unprime inlet, readily a nest of infer-
ence doubling by sequent peg, fielding the net its one untrouble of
knot. The relief comes solicited but not bright secular, goes a partial
provider of ties into lawful budding. Whose twist to free congru-
ence is by analogy the central turning space.

Gates of plantation to lineate node and unspiral its passage-crease:
devote increase to the imposition's standing cycle by storing green
fuelled asides of circle, the living cut-outs wedged square to posi-
tional ventures.

Imperforate-alert, the disturbance is tabular on frontals: fairly
deludes what can't otherwise share contour, however derived from
that assemblable *detour* unattached shade has taken *past* flow. In a
wood's light stolen not once but from off every seasonal hector of it,
repeats the wheeling intent through bare enveloped quadrisect.

Unattained as reserve in sole peripheral elation, goes centre-shade
onto that infallible code of reception, the insufficiency it deposited.

From trees in step, ghost a wood traversing interim not proving
parts at the next step: their code of analogy grazing on the open
pasture for seeing a community of centre park empty for endcase.
How a wood works to redress stoppage stirring repose beside it,
partner to its guise outside. The external pager in disparate
surround, the opening *through* trees, has not differed over incidents
of repletion, a leaf-interval homing *upon* trees.

Random stalking of analogy, but this storage-shift, close token and open requiting in common, has gone its way by no resemblance to a disencumbrance. It is but a little way to generate interactions of closure upon analogy with the insufficiency between suitable seats of states.

What is difference without amenity simples, for a wood to stock overlap under its own steps towards this lap of unplenty, unagonistic cup whether this or that alike? The dell's far rise is commonly embanked by opposite tree in tree: cover altogether there than the realm of this saver. A contrast by analogy with change but no exchange of near with far, a contingency of range regentles the fallen unfallow steps enjoining centrals.

A step is not a shadow in omission nor even the climb out of common section: as plantation fitment it seals the grade which openly insuffices the offer this side of topical furtherance. A luck of ground cut hard to belt, pawns its centre for not a little resemblance in the regression retrieval: a signal to rouse neighbours stuck to opacity-similars off solar blind.

What a neighbourhood does around the critical aspect, that secondary standing up to centre is no cross-section to itself, but the insufficiency of centre, its stable exclamation. Walking out of forests in their fellow container.

Clear robes obtain upon a distance to share: leaf-finding radiance assigns a small portion of total signal, but extended to a compound sheath unrare by impedance it cribs capacity. And observe knowns be admitted to their unnatural protection othergates across the hollow from inferred fences of light. A bareness fallen short of *direct* hollow, because wind and rain run up flush the asides.

Realism to radiant field, slowly chafing direct siting components, least-most but forest host, a decrement will not be transient when *not* affording the antagonist in plentiful indirection. Reminiscent, rather further, of completion: unique hue residue, or loci for the paying out of pastoral controls.

A diffuser plate shines *into* this sown rapidity of shadow, an earth's repudiation budget, its insufficiency project: feel it come plantational to bounds, the same connotation of world put to the same of its radiance installing correction: the grant so lessened is refraction, to instil without uncertainty a given. Asymmetry full not as a component of fall, but particles uncompliant to its non-all. Their radiance is the symmetry of less, with the entire source of collection-point. Stemmings which frighten absence, shaken for closed but give simples of insertion athirst at the retaken hoop.

The muzzle of so much at leaf-package is in work given trouble of main entirety, blunter by any universal. The outlook seems uncontingent, a centrepiece well eased by elisions of its awaiting an offence to the good: here the offhand is extra to difference in likewise unrobbed trees, markers in time to, what is no other gift to, other woods.

Plantation less in place hung on barren apparent face than a sister of the world in common: exile's insufficient shadow upon itself works to a neighbourhood of supplier shade. This woodliness going about its prescience weaves with tantrums of the good, prone to flare out its aid of nurture: the unapparent belief scolded in centrals of non-release.

An admission within the dip of light itself, its bow toward help of overhang is evening's blip at alikeness to shelter: as of light or dark, filters the here-arrived off some sharply undisguised corroboration of not-come-home. Where shelter comes to pitch in what it has not come for.

Unappeasably rutted, englutted, rocked by glade of radiant entity. A lesser which doesn't rehearse, let forward of so little other than the unsolitude of shade, the brightness of the reduct upon fellow desert.

Abstention when once encountered, but where not, never abstentive from: an absence encumbered enough to be badly encountered is the lumber of plantation's disseveral long analogy.

Living with, not to embroider the insufficiency of this wood living on where we have at once been nurtured by it. A conjunctive phantasm over-ample in displacement-spa: it will filter back on a plantation's copious occupation, what there is to fill short of, in all its leave of slanted ration.

Not inventive of the insufficiency, but co-conventional become cadent in its cone of portional light. Since consummation may not be deterred, its differing is oblique confirmation of resilient slippage of grade: but common gradient of the offer before which it is the active insufficient, space of a rotatable radiant, skimped in renewal. As this never climbs out, the gift cannot be unlearnt, much finitude as this is doesn't have projections spent in used terms of its kind. The only convertibility is desire toward unmastered receipt, the added ground less than, scarcity *within* scaled-up apposition: the torque of desire at desire's prayer still continent in insufficiency.

An injured earth unstark between pavilions real in yew or holly, in peripheral stock, central shock: this is centre resorted to, a sortal patience bestowing infill on behalf of: where the centre, as being only plantation-wide, other plantation espied, unquittingly parades its sized device for the unplanted, advice shaken only beside itself. It recedes affinities but patches the contiguities a leaf in hand across difference.

A proto-vehicle pinned to its brake, its thorn-vouch, spinning rule riven into siding, onto presiding. Human hidingness (due remotely) by pittance lit to a formalism, leaning unhollow however dropped through arch. Its patience, driven to artifice upon arraigned base, with naturalised position donning the disgrace, is fully planted up: central in cramped offer, extricably over unextractable reserve.

You would be its condolance but for straining *for* pittance. An adjunct of wood is no succession of the live wood but a meagre supersession of inscribed compass, an arrest of becoming in favour of the less become: work of plantation segment which betterment (purer woodmass) shouldn't overthrow.

This spread within cool belt sets aside recoil, opens it to a relief from shelter, if not too shy a tender of its closed body: or let be to interstices already failed elsewhere by less than local releases? Norms no roomier for what in landscape does lie to the world. Sanest streets of trees in solid.

If this duct ventures from quenched narrows, but pours *toward* similars by pinch of sustenance, it was along a green line as formerly by reparation, now by planted competition repeating the ovation. Restitution is formal, the web can be radiant in insufficiency accorded this lodge of centre: indurate bastion watches outlay to within a within of plantation, however offending entrance to trees.

How at any season the plantation is conversant with its seeds of respite, nature moulting into the wood: for this salience is as central-arbitrary in recompense, the steerage corsetting along narrow glutting: where such inclusions are technically the unhurried, difference itself goes secondary in the tranquillity of a nearer, younger difference done.

A hanging rose disconjecturing the fault in green, unseasonal or seasonless at the zonal tree to tree, joinal store, in siege of reserve.

On the spur of suffice, from this amendment cordon grant contentment its due warden. The pattern it stakes out for trees, the pittance it harbours of ease.

A shed of trees whose transparency failing among horizons witnesses what the lights' sowing may not fathom afresh: some reticent enhancer at leanest blind, unblendable, wages central-trespass, huskily scarcer than what is sifted out of it. An assimilate non-native remains formal and culls itself *until* centre, plies the vocation of an everywhere in aid between asimilars: for no longer feuding a hutment of dedication.

No sheen like human rental enamel: you force perch unsigned by anything more than plantation towards riposte.

A centre become the whereof mind assembles to its poverty. Tolerance of a gyre of plentifuls (and not so much the urban bower of depletion) has thickened this scarcity irradiant, as place performs its defeasible holism, but now upon a crop of covered surface grown too amber to be myriad calm. A single spongy cumulus encells the insufficiency of what retains: let a too-small of containment blow difficult light with universal schemes of shelter.

Local sacred of exacted measure, a facia's reserve accompanying haunt of affront: as kernel of intent the extracted intensity is deemed a factor of shrivel, no embryo. We only maltreat the guardian in you, plantation so many resentments to your times of enseatment.

Your taxed secondary layout. Centrals of it are lent for present troubles of horizontal: a fast presiding, forgiveness mooted in spot which has no transition spare from this last focal bout. Where the parallel green expects no other desertion, no more radical deserving than the taunt of plantation its inculcate intrusion.

1995–96

Landscape with Figures Afield

(1998)

The author acknowledges a considerable debt to John Dixon Hunt,
The Figure in the Landscape (1976)

Here, in a remote, preparatory and instrumental working, imposition is dedicated to the woods.

Knots and compartments, whose speculations are matched to a helper of root: lest this green world is not sufficient to look abroad into the fields.

Cascades amend, but fail to tend, a broken world: you certainly incline the leaning of a wall to naturalism.

Apparent spoil, but no waste of the irreparable reaches.

The duty of mutual strife with ground: where a break in the branch has twisted onto a root.

An unsolitary world does but transliterate other worlds.

Not to concede a probable nature, so as not to exceed a parlous one.

To picture the fields as mere variety leads our expectations into the city, to a theatre of repentance.

A variety to chance the mind's own multiplicity, round a narrow compass to purge the rectitude of finitude's entirety.

Nature's *incurious* accuracy: that some casual truths call for a measure of addiction is not injurious.

Accidents of clouds over a city do not omit the rains of regularity.

Art's exuberance chastened by silence: this is not art reducible to an avidity of no noise.

Every stick planted to some purpose: every stone laid over some purpose.

A self-taught abstract, by time immersed in a vast wood, the plantation of it no unavailing formality if it learn of a glade opening.

A retentive mind out of sorts distinguishes no varieties of moss.

Attentive individuals are not singled out, not distracted by too inquisitive a contrast in the crowd's eye.

The mind opening is diffusive of harmony, but does not disperse what it opens upon.

With frequent foot to answer the weather, nurtured by mourning having ceased, a cessation careless as solitude.

The oncoming of spring treasures the analogies of neglect sufficiently tended: responsibilities can but range from one season to the next.

Specificities are without exception, but not the known marks of exemption.

The *explorable* inaccessible, when the forest doesn't darken round, but accords amazement *to* ground.

Dispose carefully about the lower landscapes hints to tempt the non-various into an absence which is cautious.

A broken landscape roughs it out, to follow the rigid incline in the hills.

Diversity without character is variousness without altitude.

What pursuing, once interrupted, will continue on to the pause?

If, at an involuntary pause, the mind is struck by its own character, it may become a matter of temperament to pursue the involuntary.

A seat within a knot, a thorn-bush within a grove.
Attentive to imploration if all's well in no other woods.

No embowering raid on the stationary could move your pausing eye.

What cannot literally be accounted variety are figures at home in their different landscapes.

See the fading many in the valour of the woods.

Through the saddened grove, where scarcity is hard toil, fears the woodman.

The mixing passions eschew scenic variety to bind their compounds to slower encounters.

The meanings of retreat are a public in dialogue which can be *heard*.

I don't claim from the human the power to purge the human: I claim for the human the natural debt of unseemly belonging.

Lavish directions demand nature but with something in hand.

The maze signifies an apparent labyrinthine contrition: a more patient regret is suffered as far as the centre.
Palings are avoidable but not empty: never leap fencing directly, never clear space indirectly.

It is not the horrid which engages with wilderness, but an unwrought grace of the mind: unmade by that very dedication, a gift of trepidation.

Art respects nature's own usury: something owed is dedication in the raw.

Winding the cloth of woods along a deep valley, through which you hatch the long reach of winter.

Our singing for keels overtuned the strings of the woods.

Only a landscape can be certain what *are* the accidents of nature.

The shape of a landscape is made with the non-human, materials not composed for a logic of occupation alone: which is to say, history speaks more fluently where it only irregularly fills a landscape.

The descent into some hollow of ground serves to instil a void on which thought might have its fill. How the land's contours were gradually smoothed away.

When figures emerge from their landscapes, what intention do they presume to resign?

To imagine the good of imprecision is to allow too little of a composition to be withstood.

'Half a tree' may overtake a subject, but is way off course for the object.

A complaint disastered, if it turns on a plea for unsimple scope.

A scope prematurely encompassed, if it has no pliancy reposed in it.

The minimal is refusal, or diffusion post-thematic, a universal because leaving out only one world at a time.

Catch thyself with landscape: swiftly thwart imagination's virid eye, by the woods lonely not lulled.

Tending the hint, giving the mind a composed turn, rarely hurrying the futile, sparing the 'nothing lost'.

'Wildish largest' groves—a long way from aspiration.

A broken scene checks our desire not to shrink from it: diminished courage has the quieter eye before due lessening.

Genial presentiments: a chastened *furens* will not denature unhastening *locus*.

What is it answers to feature in the minds of the possessors of venture?

Passion in me longs for things of a natural kind: genuine order is the primitive breaking in on the primitive.

A landscape of configured naturals: so much across the infinitely alive, and at least between finite uprights not for the living alone.

Whitefield in Wild Wheel

(1998)

Preface

Whitefield Clump is a small, elongated landmark-plantation estab-
lished on the top of Ibsley Common in the 1830's, not far from its
southern declivity. The Avon valley looks up from the west and the New
Forest stretches unbrokenly away to the east (the Common is now
incorporated into the Forest). I have known the outline of these trees
for much of my life, but always thought the clump too plain and rudi-
mentary to be possible to write about—a token huddle increasingly
ragged in recent years; it was never a productive or significantly enter-
able inclosure, still less a remnant of ancient woodland. I usually
spotted it on its hill-slope from the south but over the last few years I
have got to know it better from across the flatter (though fissured)
heaths to the north and north-east, and now think of it more as a cyno-
sure to lure a walk round, linked to a circuit rather than to an ascent.
As such, Whitefield pulses and attracts, often confusingly reticent
about its true configuration: sometimes supposedly circular and
almost Janus-like in symmetry, while a bit further on it will appear
oblique and foreshortened, or at another point flatly linear like an
overgrown hedge on the skyline. There are no fences but it's uncom-
fortable to linger inside—you feel immediately drawn out again
towards that distended immediacy which seems to wheel beyond it.

What is it walks into circle in any eking-out of refuge but doesn't
stay upon shelter as such? The poem is haunted by the figure of wheel-
ing, discovering a familiar haunt in a new way once the attraction
seems not so much at the heart of it but wheeling outside it. The poem
explores how that outside / inside might be set aside or set beside by a
wheeling. Whitefield Plantation emerges not so much as feature, but
in terms of what makes a circuit round it, a circle burdened by an
attraction to site, but leaving no mark. Who or what wheels, the poem
cannot say, though it knows what can be carried in the motion, and
the terrain is definite enough (if no longer quite in terms of a "sense of
place"); so also is the formal passion of the encircling, however inde-
terminate the radius.[1]

I come to Whitefield as a wood which breaks off from containment
with the sullen poise of a fragment around which any asymmetry is no
longer singular but must wheel. What does seem like an absolute is the
sense of a touch or spot as something reservedly (rather than subver-
sively) *less* than its own constituents, the wheeling of a place tracked in
some other way than through the patterning of its own particles. A

pittance of beginning comes to be a place's round, drawing towards what can be offered on its behalf, so that something of itself touches upon mourning as wheeling which overlays any emblematic circle, but not so as to privilege movement over stasis, since this is a movement haunted or traumatised by a *deflective* closure, *ie* a stasis not quite on its own territory. These are the elements of what I think of as a flow-cycle, but it won't go into purely ecological terms because the cysts and grits of an emblematic recall have contaminated it, becoming inseparable from what wheels rather than swirls.[2] There is a sense of scarcity (very much available to a mourning for environmental degradation) which takes to itself an emblematic brittleness, one below renewable relations but here given access to a degree of core around which what is scarce does renew in a non-indifferent (if not reconstructed) way[3]. Where this scarcity might be thought to transmit revival, it is as an arena of nurturing reserve, but it doesn't amount to a web which spins an infilling texture; rather, what is occupiable about it wheels round it. To look at it another way, I can imagine material granulations (especially when shorn of organic accretion) spontaneously give rise to symbolic emergences or consistencies. For scarcity is the difficulty and frugality of relation, or what laps the natural and symbolic, but which, as scarcity, ensures that such a switch-over is always on but always partial in its transfers, which is also to say any difference is *impure* across scarcity's narrow commons. Frugal relations don't supervise a unitary structure but if shared spaces or pairings of domain do occur as a matter of adaptive or empirical economy, it is because scarcity can't afford the constant vigilance which an expense of primal plurality seems to demand. It is how scarcity can be imagined, then, as a source of plentiful analogy, or what a non-fullness never actually negated or dispersed can be *for*. It is an instinct of this poetry that what opens onto any schematic absence in fact rigidifies—for me the enigmatic statics of wheeling better maintain a negotiation with limit-attraction (limit as exchange of attachment across domains but not the plurality of domains as such) amid the pain of a detracted or no longer fully functioning organic centre[4].

Wheeling is also a hunger for commemoration, the sort of spatial inscription which though authorless on the ground does write on behalf of, at the friction-point of its local attraction. The recall is cooler and scarcer for being in the round. This doesn't absolve the wheel from ghosting a version of obsessional magnetic homing across fragmentary arrays of virtual desert: but as such it can approximate to (in readmitted organic terms) a sustainable motion, to a reservoir of attachment breathing itself outward, onward, surrounding what is an uncoupled hub amid a swirl of rota by love. We can't enlarge our exceptions (the poetry of love reduced to scarcity, or loss itself, is not the *same* as absence): we do only shift the point of scarce dependency, not as beyond but further round (though scarcity itself accesses a moment of transcendence), ravelling up the incidents of our life on the turn, but where in this history there is no next turn in terms of swerve or acceleration. But where exception in the forms of break-out or transformation is temporarily (and so writably) exhausted or wounded, there can be an atemporal commemoration, bridling up against its horizon, but offering something to that horizon from within a scarce difference of connection and retention. It is the two together perhaps (dynamic offence in time and a symbolic perfection of damage out of time) which eventually take up the flow, a flow of retentions but in which broken retentions flow. Paradoxically, in terms of any dedication, that flow *has* to be taken up even though here it arises from its power to wound us involuntarily. It reduces our reconciliatory aspirations (towards a rediscovered sense of dependency) to the condition of scarcities: but we take up what flows by means of the resource of scarcity, the para-organic enclave of wheeling, a wheeling for the wild.

Notes

1. I am reminded of Geoffrey Hartman's comment on *The Ruined Cottage*: "Yet we glimpse already a centrifugal movement, which encompasses more in nature than specific place, and whose shape approximates a circle". *Wordsworth's Poetry* (1964), p. 137.

2. Rather than dissolve this emblematic plaque, it is here allowed to figure as a wheeling, not literally arrested but nonetheless dynamically held in thrall. It is the *attached* residue of something sacral, but tenacious now largely by reason of contamination. The excrescent ring might then be a site of offering or unburdening in a way which doesn't dissolve itself back to a healing flow, but retains its (infected) girding around fidelity to a spot, even though that fidelity is now only valuable as an offering. An offering to what? Probably to what lies outside the immediate history of feeling and association which has marked but not sufficiently renewed a landscape, which if it has an ecological future at all, can't be aligned (who knows whether it's an expansion or contraction?) along that sort of sense of place. But where else could this be thought or said? An offer, then, by virtue of its entanglement, at least within this cycle . . .

3. The "ruin" of which Hartman speaks (see note 1 above) in my poem perhaps threatens to be nature itself, but in the mourning associated with the wheeling, ecological ruin is both ghosted and exorcised. If nature were literally ruinous, this could not finally be symbolized culturally. Such a sense of place swollen with loss would revert to just another accretion, whereas what wheels round that centre is not only focal but also *thins* out the density of conventional place.

4. See Hartman again: "A fatality of centre persists and defies definition . . . at [the] centre is something too central: fixed and scarcely human". *Op cit*, pp. 137–8.

1: Prelude

There is no *stretch* in avoidance ending, save at the wheeling. Where a place of extinguished compass is at large across sheerer keeping, in despite of accrual.

Not yet an edge feeding outlet through space, or ground to a shore upon surface. Given that for wheeling a plantation was to be at stake. A cluster of stems finds the offence rota agrees to fixity, dropping from reach a lustreless axile.

An anchorage force which pillories drift to thin course, though a furnished clamp will not have limped out to it. If receptacle is to be the abstainer, too much travelled across, amplitude wheels aversion's winning an effusion for limits.

What comes of the split in stasis is the axle pitted to haul short of wheel. The wheel of attraction it discharges onto, once the place is bereft by what is less than a movable part of itself.

Points affixedly world-sparse await its wheeling fund, the stunted originary target. Physically lost (hounded) onto position but reforwarded in a wheeling unladen towards reliance.

Place wheels when there has been a turn at the unlimited from off its appalling centre: a twist neat-bid for fragment, not iteration. In unlike defts, so as not to wheel them merely like the unlike.

As darts of landing, thrown to a parti-position of slender strike, prick radially flat upon a wheel's shallow time.

Surrounder of the contentions panned to dead-scarce hub of the turn. Pinned apart at the spot which spins them the sames by which they aren't still.

A small land whose islands of rod seem concentrated without substrate, but that pinching sub-status deemed fragmentary, and grateful again with wheeling.

This place is the bordering of central orders for dismissal, no enclosure lidded enough to lift its own unaccretive given out of wheeling. A wheeling to grounds without attainment, were it not for a loved scarcity of occupancy.

No auspicious desertion of the lessenings of place, it wheels desert across the holding, seals in scarcity a wheeling otherwise unstirring. According diminishment a scale of relief, across which the assault had cycled to survive.

In preparation of crushed bond. Confer removal rates that tend to this clip storage.

Not returning, but turning round a centre stultified on source, flaked pivotal as course. What screens resource from linear indifference *houses* the stultification.

Bestrewal pinned at less-than-whole in the round, given what is broken aid from. Continual berthing, unnumerous recharging: retreat recedes the scarcity, wheels it this side of future receipt.

Bare taxing of horizon unnaturally requited by things wheeling in place. Trustful infinities of departure before a shared origin of untended finitude. Too focal for any more distance than at wheeling remove. To have changed out of series, replete in its phantom of transfuge, or where a plain refuge flattens wheeling's sky.

Scarcity never attains void, owing to a scurf of originary compression, a garth of unwinding diminishment. Where too rich a space would be leeway it cannot put to, a passage not nimbly hurt onto ground.

What is normal in place is its broken sanction as location, relational model de-limbed, excluded from lateral expedition. A norm the fragment betokening it will skim from cloak, but not revoke.

Dependent *for* scarcity on what will rotate about it lessened by too little of the far: does not *imperfectly* oscillate like a more vantaged mourning.

Becalming the stigma of a point which is everywhere studded by position. It is wheeling unpunctured by root which does the embedding.

Poverty as space, wound on refuge, both defect from wild tenuity: as protective a breadth of weightlessness in the wheeling.

Its tracking a limit across loss offended what affordance there is for a radiant deficit to contribute in spin, until poorly it turned resplendence loose on the neck of the wheel.

Extension is that after-tension of token verity occurring to a place's present brief in wheeling. Less by sleight of remission that what it is a scarcity can be *of*: impure dimension, numinous ruts of completion.

Struck distances wheel the short flaws of time, generative depletion engages gyrostatic churn: not enough to fill but by ward to chart obtainer.

It attempts to picket a world in plenary session, the place pocket. Things of ruin which liked nature to be their own. Locked for a scope of earth and minding its no-container: pinioned to the tug of it, wheel it wild what recovers blank arts of the wide.

Non-essential cohesion will not benumb, for compressive accord, a wheeling of the ordinary. Unimmensely limited, gratefully extended, healing onward from mere weave the ensuring wheel.

2: The Clump

Whitefield's feckless regency of attached range, the slicing of radials perfectly pitches at a local completion's reel: from ache of tissue this assent to steal out core.

A centre begins when a place inapplicably belies place, when subversion of ground indurates and inaugurates.

A plantation without rides, unridden on belt, the weal of change doesn't marvel tightness until hunted on regional circuit. It flies at pivotal implacement from out of scarce preform, no middle assembly, no aisle among later ways.

Whitefield, the proximate is finished with you, not so numerous in uprights as numinously beacon-prone.

Unprescinded but raked to narrow precinct by small grounds of it, the windcrack steals into brake, finds the bringing shock right for the belt it makes, what eventual placation scarcely decides: poor locus resides an inveterate wheeling *from*.

So galled, the pine is pebble pitched into wheel from deficit tangle. A stone's site may be rolled on by woods, any throw is fate of wheeling round trunks of stony parity: the order not to strike off from such favouring unrarity.

No hearth denies the shell of itself, pieces which do branchtips won't surrender to place their sparks of scarcity: not splinters put to rival ground but sinking it in less than striking any rock of reduction: without root-touch it is they ignite the dearer wheeling done.

Green local sending moments, strength envelope of discrete pittance.

The clump is ghostly clearance, amassing outward what is beamed missing to concentric session.

Not bowling to rim, but wheeling assimilation in spite of not gone to holder, in light of the clump's unretirable mask on outpour.

To expend any sudden rest in the abiding is first to nest a strand of squat firs in the unconfiding.

Rigid sub-body is the normal hooding, precompression likes this not to have deposed in a wood. Scarceness in finding focuses a tremor of provision, around whose sorted rarity a plenary of segments shares denial.

A clump is absolute socially with inherent stake, not astringent skin but revolving towards exterior, exposed so far as the outside wheels. And the leavings-in are the wheel of the floor, store no more than brought to stow, broadest of less than enough enwraps the tapering of enough: turn with the deficit spurned-to.

Whitefield: not holding in but fragmentary scold on pin, the impenetrant sharp function decries incompletion. Not to wheel round this clump would be to rely on its featurelessness.

A knot of trees is imposition on which the unabsorbable revolves by nature, what is full-grown gathers to itself its non-victories. Place would be that traject-position known by its arcs not to slight victims.

The clump beseigingly embodied is slower than coherent particle, but puts relief occupation to the turn. A plantation capped: not for a surrounding surface but the heavy chance of a wheeling surround.

The core unincurred, wheeling round it uncured of a reservoir of besettings. Primarily round these few uncontaining stakes, their blunt cut into the unweathered open.

No entry loop but a detraction of branch as direct charge upon the open, seeding the space from any spate of freeing the open. Nurture on screen-infill turning nature through each vision of insufficient inclusion.

Nearness at a thirst for the near-hooded, it steers a splinter of place wooded, this will face generous state on the wheel.

Bare facia begged at unenterable plantation, an empty room shuttered in shadow deduction where walls are hung from captious furniture, no apparatus of passage. A swinger to shelter will rival enough boom, believe in the round how its welter of the unalterable stretches to reconnoitre.

So many tentative stiffnesses in variety to a web of space, a glancing fixity's partitive assembly, it trembles inked apertures unslight in their pause, scarce light upon which to scratch apart.

Not welling up through sticks of it, written out by rotation self-sparred, the here of it cannot be underfoot: in its sub-repletion underway a star of centric remission.

At NW the prow: pines flag-up, turn their windburn *onto* the wind which sifts no more than this: direct forecastle is for trees to go about, disenroot the keel's force: but will be now, in rank, times further divisible as may curve into the many more invisible.

Whitefield, your cells of plenitude muster consensus at scarcity, at what gives omission to what the defences do, piked for a convexity of poor root: to shuffle the fidelity of all such non-betweens.

Your understorey browsing on entasis of pineframe, by pinelet winning lift for itself: but dependent on cartage, replacement is a load too light to rise, unsealing a furrow of bony light slenderer than the young in shade. From it a whole semi-vacant parent frame is sprung.

Resurgence is for bruise of formals, but beneath a bleach of over-stand whose own breach of event is the more careful make-less of formulaic dues. Renewal of skeleton is green unemergent thrift piling a shell it can no longer unenforce: because bones of the reliction are seconded to cycle without infringing on surf.

Elasto-drastic, the release complies an indifferently containable self: sooner left astraddle in bandying of bones than turn the site's spindle throughout dilational well: wherever an unstationary residual swerves to fission in beseech of rigid lurch.

Uplit housing, but least thin to sky, the windshield host rising heavier than hollow, the printed spin of it writing off protruding ghost, the arc in post.

How the site will wheel enough to lend out local stress, and such is leaf-string, though may a tree end unhorizoned by it under load. Gone the true way of sprung calm.

A still-point sorrowed from another order, or harrowed by one which cannot drive the border, and narrowed for what doesn't dole but borrows back to primal obstination: whose unfilterables are set cementable into the open cycle.

The place postpones a region to its pin, its sharp drop to cover will not have local bundles abstain, they remain to be thickened by what unprovidently wheels: by which aggregate its things are no longer the bane of their own rest.

3: A Fragment Striates

At fragmentary nexus snapped degrees trap sticks—with no starker quittance than this. A light breakdown into conspicuousness cedes its series halt to the familiar.

Ubiquitous centre scotched into emissory event by the impassage of fragment. The quotient poll of itself will not even crowd out circle.

The place of the clump alters its distance round whatever particle it finds fallen to poor casing. Foreshore of impact seeds what there is of distance to wheel.

The incurved windshell has trees peel off encasement where there is no other cordon to toil with it: some shards are bodily rounds through to static pliability, an ample cramp receptive at fault.

This fragment of plantation is a shifter fallen into the rift of its beacon indication, plugged to a landscape's parings by blockage of switch: the turn to wheeling.

Rock-full of loss but earthen of that less which a particle stocks: from the cyclic intervals in absence it will avail linear exit only so far wrapped, stilting a furtherance at wheel.

The outrun is scarcity by section thinned circuit-damp at centre, sparing it for a parasitic encompassing, or until dry by fealty of wheel: infinity no longer hunts the hub itself.

The severals without spite, righted in compatible wheeling, hold towards this plantation less than one complete thing: a particle of shell from the centre outwards in sole replete apparency of wayless ring.

Engroundment finds out an acumen of silt: fragment is longer than itself the tether, no slenderer lodging than this is broken off into reminder miles of hold.

Not a piece of shape but a fragmentary extent of no supply, other than the wheeling is no longer alone with its motion.

Inhabitation rationed to steadiness at port, not weaving the fasting huddle but wheeling out to what will visit it unfitted to vaster entry. To place fragment is to run with parasitic spread, how a clump enables its unrenewed. And confine these connective scares to a spurt over radials until urged by a concentric askance. Unstolen fragment will daily string out an interior this glad.

The fragment may not go lateral, gone to littering the accident's adhesion as subaltern of ruin sweeping the non-empty. A fixity of quasi-wreckage abuts radials of the sullen gleam, shredless before ungreetable, what wheeling cheats nowhere within turn.

A void cannot exist without body, but has no manner of clearance subsisting within fragment. What it is that steering for the body abandons, but nowhere dear, left for home.

What avoids a snapped boundary newly thrown on limit is genuine concision of multiple body: no fragment breaks at sheer crux, its jointure falls *with* it to a break in time, the welt of it goes to seed the turn about crux.

A scene scanted across clump put to scheme. The outward calamity a reversion from the unskeined. The wheel no longer tortical where a surround has no supplementary, all is dis-opened by fragmentary patience.

What could circle the crush to a less than either: jarred figment of shelter dropped off passage, or a pinned wheeling ajar?

Fragment falls behindhand with the *unlocated*, thickens empty autonomy of site towards heaviest shedding yet upon its own patrol around insufficiency. Acceleration unabsorbed but alerted to being starved by drive, that slow wheel outside focal obstacle.

Veiled fragment spiked to space but barely unstill at its wheeling.

Not quite the void where you need it, but a branchless displacement plugging purely emergent avoidances: shall seed projection, being plugged, but only along the striation of what breaks from trees.

A stopped pore ruins the rarification, is plundered for its spoilt solid until pivotal. Near-flung disgrace until tampered in modal fragment far-knit.

No place can be neatness together of both brace *and* welter. Wheeling spurns any fostering of foisted reach if not spilt for its depthless tread, if not fixedly ill at a forest in fragment.

In this cellular lapse, space relays confessed time, the fragment quails the place at its impounded juncture with domain: a siphon of plenitude, abridgement across hierarchy, it wheels scarcity round the very connaturals which differently abate: equate no desert swirl with desertion.

The need for real as a fall off scale, scalded fold which can't slide to a further field but is arrest at the break itself: it speciates by a refusal of all but wheeling. So sharpen the vexed instant of shedding, thin-host real-cycle embedding.

Receptively lean of conjunction where parts fall into stress of store no other members are. But wheel the empty plenty of a field *not* sparked by the dense squall of a fragment touching off centre.

Material plenum pinned to arrivals/compliances by brittle reassembly, the sheddings at a rate of space: not around pivot, but what is read *as* pivot of insufficiency.

Can export immunity from gap only as what is unfillable at proportion of network: then to invariable community, non-ramification on the wheel of it.

Unless without, no scar on silt, no one-more-lessened diversity to propose to one another's frugality in the open pattern of adjustment. Wheeling a scarce universal, its close score in unreproducing fragment.

Binding below provision takes to a ground, at this scarcity rotates, wheels rather than embeds the recovery. Not vestige but figment brushing leaf forward, nobody's leave clapped into the kindness cell.

Drawn round what is nothing to fragment other than how mere it is unwithdrawn. This wheeling outside a primordial will be taxed with what the punctilium of reserve cannot ask.

Factional enough for axis, the fit is detractable centration: as micro-striate numbly adheres to co-reserve, its own lenticular argument doesn't wheel.

Weaned of a central accident the community stands by its rootable reductions. Where a spent focus leans, the resting is wheeled continuum, district noise of wreckage adrift from a negative. The sift is lessness made over to pastoral truncation, that other rind there will be in a slighter denial.

Gathers for its own obstruct the unnaked fragment coated with jointure intact, but attacked with a poverty of direction which hasn't risked what wheeling has finished plentifully without it.

To hold which pilots itself from fulfilled debris of limit. Wheeling itself no such edge, it is when rotation is trampled corona.

A universal screened by fragment, scarcity's girding shines now in rehearsive germ, but amid wheeling greater done by a lesser refusal at one. Great statics wheel, thick alone for the near things, mediately shorn of fragmentary veer.

4: With Wheeling Economy

No wheeling is immense beyond pleasure, this *is* measure if its proto-horizon rectify close enough for fragment. The moment of uncamoflaged protection not pressed home, arisen wild at the rumour of thickening interior.

Loosed to closure (wheel wide)
from dilation of springhead,
toporeversal is face of dearth
arraying its nurse-quake in circuit

Spectral clemencies for
domains whose point singulars
wheel, spared elliptic border

Traject solely traced off
circus, stirring tracks
from primitive rejectory,
the common room in re-
exospore, abstrict in fit,
singles their caveat of home

heft of weather-take-body
weft less tether-sate-orbit

Wheeling is grace on perimeter but an otherness of confinement unrepleatable in what is not yet another piece of place, but in direct glue of asymmetric fragment. The same boundless space wheeling poorer rounds.

The wheel leaves no rind to deposit endlessness on, but for like impurities drew close to the trees' spine.

To give joint to slippage, its wheeling fund rips succession from all but the rigid figures of its point of turn: a sudden salience on the wheel of recall.

Imperfect limit-norms, dripping within fit their swell-like lessness, devolving the roam of the bounded. What spins is limit not limit to the same things.

Wheel in the midst of what has cut into encompassing, holding out not as null body but as lull in the particle protending.

So little circumselective but axially speculative, wheelings are the inclusion its expanse doesn't afford tended by a break into centre. How the open is neglected once encasement gets stubbed out on the one wheel always before horizon: that circuit-dark readily appearing to the shade of a broken object.

What turns is outcome acting for brief distance recursive by enchantment: what is stinted is how little reduction is needed to tie an apt impoverishment round the neck, by slowest tree-provision, of origin.

Wheeling, to no value in pursuing, the thin corridor of the ingredient: stir sidelessly, but screened in outcurve from a *solitary* decay into centre.

Conjoint venture as in fragment laid rare, by its scarcity full tour upon the surrounders our unexplorable neighbours in plenitude, leanest coming round into relation.

Free-running birch across the open hill ever younger into thinning, their expulsion allowance unspun. Outfliers of cluster on other business to ground, these silent equalities of solo puncture are less wild, more immobile, than the wheeling itself, its ageless conferral scar of attraction.

Circling doesn't skirt bad shores from the outer leaves, lighter disgrace is to be had in the purer shelter-hem itself: brilliant breeze-less reserve of what sets eternal dome far enough within to resort to wheel.

For frail paralysis of accommodation the clump is fuelled at circle, or how an exhaustless plume is not crossed for having been smoked out to cycle.

The leaves will have tailed a wry, non-ingestive wheel, curtal of sacral for free detail, complete warning's local patience. Easy trueing of turn aligned on weakness of bond.

A single infection to spare beyond cluster, uncurable by release: the healing will not be partial, but neither is it within slip-range of the feed chamber it respects. A pressure scene still a less than provided, but guiding wheeling where no locality can prise off the edge.

Regioning knocked to region-ring as butt of primal insufficiency: not sole for surface but sweep of face layering reaped surface. From its deep abbraded outlay it broached wheel to be the layer of it.

Relegated to circling in the glow of unrepeatable punishment, draws up preoccupied conciliation of the one remove: coil a single stay. No length in wheel other than companion time of the one space out: diurnal relay, lonely observance upon a foundational crowded spot, quietened by the shareables of scarcity.

Unevenly, this receptacle hesitates with diverse nurture until assured the path winnows *towards* obstacle, merely lightening all in its curve.

A channel for any current knack of obliteration, whose starving assuages the swerving: enough of little restored without little to end, only so much defeat in quest. It vies with the heterogenous to be its *own* given to a properly unpossessed.

As though ungrasping limits could circumvacate. Action is ambient, not recaptive of hold: from hold's blank comes a span of wheel that holds off, as cycle, from avenging the blunted by provision.

As if wheeling round little more than a mired limb can assume other rites bridge this place. The infinite of it is its inoperative necessity, its resting shallow, a dance of reserve not encumbered enough to uncage what is wild in wheeling to outworn storm, promised forgotten siege.

Whose ties are divisive *unless* they wheel, whose bonds undo by all the arrival they attract *once* they wheel.

Calm is the wheel if it wend circuit, rested from nature upon an earthed circum-event: unbranching hub, spokeless to print out nomalous core, avocal as the inwardness.

And bad clump not to have frequented some comliness, until few enough *are* trees, as when unrequited by aura they don't scatter. They are surrounded, at stark scenic biddance.

Wheeling at less than pure passage, this not-continuing seen to be nearly unowned beyond. But no impersonation of wheel by what is near only since a perfect interruption mimicked the unbroken. The wheeling of it isn't habitable.

Wheel isn't feature, but feature's turn to a naturalised instruction. Defection from within reverted dispersal: erase the postern when the latch is cycles, foreshorten horizon but do not indent.

These things explain their lingering upon chastening, the scrape-limits evolve from a scrap of origin. That screen of dejected purchase juts through this annexe of setting forth: no farther interception on the wheel.

Precariously condensed, it will cleave to common domain in the round, at what remove attraction settles it: enwrap in less than static grass, but in full resistance spin the stop. Striven for in crusty bleedings of attachment fed a plaque at cursus.

Rolling is scarce mechanism, staffed without floor. Its turning-rod is at least cheap to the rare, imperfect against numinous embrace.

5: Love's Plenary Analogy

A scant base wheeling, at a parch of not closing down, stalked by solace towards outcoil in figment: or claims openness for relimits along a spine of attraction, is within coming to the contoured lips of it.

It is not as not at all, but brightly scarce, opening to scale. The containing was non-causal, intact fabric cast forward from its fasting centre.

Or broken if the one thing *lighter* than dispersal, the not-there in its perfect round, but in breach weighted to absorptive gyration. Outside enough within which, relay isn't come for linear speed, uniquely abstaining from the fastnesses of centre.

The wreckage is wry outcome that these same things resemble full generosity to: what doesn't affirm fragmentary recovery in any struck 'imperfect' array of it.

The convex impurities won't have given wrong matter to fragment, they swell the attachments whose demeanness scored onto lenient zone, regioning well of the fainter satieties.

Attracted to wheeling stead is what is there to spin out from saturated starving board, no longer so starkly seated either beside attraction's hesitant own. Less than a moving part vesselled in a fragment's arc, sank by circle to the still. From unknown stillness the wheeling is known.

Something granted when garnered at the disjoin, a planted for less clarifies the tissue of relation, and, as not concluded, shall not have reached out unbounded.

That the bodily aura invests by its scarcity any most intimately leaving part of an antecedently separated world.

Precise personifying, rings of earth ally the primitive additive but turn upon scarcity. Not to deserve this loving ground condition, one of reach, but how to liken its offer, impair fidelity with wheel?

Sheered wheeling of a love not proud enough in time to die of a pure set of place in change. Induced, it quits for less than iterative convolution, but where wheel is still too poor for crescent swerve. Offend in unbroken curve precipitate motes of love entered by bents in time: lodgement let into mourning's motion when memory out-turns steeper end by quotient of space spent.

Adversity countersunk at a microtopic prone to make test of loss: not joining frontiers by defeat but drains by reserve contortion, gritted on shards of rest.

Flexural stillness amplified, grown roundly stopped, an insufficiency of furnishing hampered by slight touch into tightness of love: which earth wheels for guidance past abstention, gaining in it the outright fallow of a clump.

This absorptive partiality is particle for central bane, a contemplative nodule ingresses the alien path bud-shelled toward locus.

Gang-wheeling a thin elopement from section, Whitefield clump at cost, by sensitive cause paying for courses. Love rounds on benignity despite immersive inter-rapture, this is not to fine unincluded things: but is what rotates its incast splinter-shelter, if history became warmth the dipping now is unerased feature, cooler than horizon.

To find presageful zone, the peace of its landing, upon neglected emotion, though the wheel is consistent to interested pain: spins it withstood but not withdrawn from the unlit attraction.

Rota of no addressable you once love dispartners attentively, its source a division by symmetry-mistake, a lesser of two selves wheeling. No longer scarcity's *core*. An interruptive compass wheels badly within means. Keeping the spot accorded familiar glow stepping back from itself into mere place, the congested patterns of the less.

The scratch of a call goes cellular, faith does poor ground of removing it here, cycled upon scratch it is overload tented unnomadic, striated to within an outside contour of attachment: as though common tour will smooth out the catchment without abandoning it.

It gives grace to itself without being correctly turned, wheeling beside the opacity of attraction, long gone into the offering love it became plenteous by: iteration is light of cycle, unrefinable until *not* a non-return.

There is no difference to receive, a not-otherwise distributes the change into scarcity.

Mourning at single coil, a policy of mourning has no labyrinth at rim, its simple turn by one dimension doesn't spiral attrition as the other's dove of readmission. Misquoted from grief, attraction mutates its fall to a different fully-alone, field-born of remembering insufficiency by arena. From unabsence broken in pair to unsolitude's prevailing on scarcity.

What plight of catchment is a love unresumed but consumes by lateral fervour, when waves of georelation march its break over scarce appointment? Where wheel is passing love from love, within the loved-awhile but not as from love *to* love.

Chisel a fragment of pacification, needle together direct agreement circling the unrequired self but not defaced by resolution to tree orbit. This resurfaces beneath love's temporal inconformity, its mistake about sustainability amid other communities the after-time animates. Infirmity when pruned to a local attractor compresses out onto a fidelity circuit too indigent for latitudes of deformity.

Being without you has crashed the nucleus of your departure, so far as a crowning of the uncontinued by wheel. The out-turn is attach-ment-broken, haunted by pure pattern of a refusal to break *with* attachment: the spaces rest in adherent speculation given that what leaks through fusion is only horizon. Though loss was not a resident accident, attachment elects it now as poor station which all the micro-congruents amplify: the slightness of its love-adja-cency is the bend in centre swarming to plight.

Love no taller than a point of entry, shrivelled to a kernel in the round, as a community of the widest desire is propped abjuringly. It serves by cycle this body no oftener conjoined, no longer truly extricated part from part, but press excess to the wheeling.

Mourning tours the exit-base vouched for by fragmentary pro-union: the relata don't quote break along the same flaws they join.

A snaring into bestrewal with no suppliant of entity to share surplus: the excess was in bringing such scarcity to bear.

The body has formed of its late element a compression member, sprung to a date of encirclement: in the nothing put by it would be easy to fear revival, but this is not a visitation in its own company, not set to rounds by any union of chamber.

Everything is to slake storm at its normal fording of zone, as in a rival serenity, were it not to risk raging for survival outside the scarcity of serenity itself.

But here some rectilinear magnet of the event-scape is little in little surrendered: where scarce is to hold as surround is to an openness fed boundary at its daily sundered history.

An awakenable crescent-at-hand to conserve the inaffordances of earth, oblique equity is excess railing at bleakness, a subfigure lean of us: to attune unrequital to touch, its fragment-table set amid key vocational rigidities.

The infinity of it does end at a slighted crust of the unceasing, in finite allay to accomplish similar goaded wending, practises at cycle a dearth tending its deserted information: planing out to where the out-won spoil is not succession, but a niched diurnal of scarcity's prayer remeant end on end.

How to conclude, and now to reserve, extravagant targetting of a subdued? To round on its world is to circle it nearer than what occurred *for* it, but beseeches its spares in one.

It *is* enigmatic if love has caused itself out without being able to cross the span: reliance is the crater sworn to raze all but curve and more scarcely here than it is greater. Availing the common cluster by aching eternals, a few trees pooled externally clear of groundless deeming, pulled-to in plentiful encirclement.

June 1997–March 1998

Spirit of the Trees

(1999)

Acknowledgements

The poems printed here are selective reworkings of poems drawn from a 1947 anthology called *Spirit of the Trees*; my versions adopt a stanza form consisting of seven lines of seven syllables—the form suggested to me by Peter Riley's *Small Square Plots* (1996) and offered here in tribute. The titles of the source-poems are retained, and the original author's initials are recalled beside each title.

The Beech Tree's Petition (TC)

Fruits are my unwarming shade.
Bright wintry childhood murmurs
honour seen barren-beechen,
vows a gloss of summer spent
by my trunk's sportive altar:
spare rapture survives in hive,
carve its bud on bloomless frame!

To a Dead Tree (GNC)

Sterile in your shadow hope
you possess there relentless
semblance of the gentle, death
enchanting the garden art-
ifice of breath: bud or tear
in equal nest bestow sapped
leaf on colonies of end.

The Elder Tree (WC)

Lamp-thick with white flower, an
aspiration will eye the
spell in hide, like day glimmer
cool cave onto the shut of
white, dwell pale-cloud then flood
the smiling slowly home, occur
lonely past milken twilight.

Morning, the Sixteenth Day (RC)

This garden beneath a twig
attacks prophecy, I mind
to add another sign leaf-
ing the ravage of event:
tread core until pliable,
serve out its change at under-
foot, at shall I fill the need?

The Wych-Elm (RC)

In weariness of rumour
bitter with musing, I tire
a world apart, labour of
boughwhip forages my leaf:
green sham put on human door,
the house murmurs below branch,
trembles for share of neighbour.

The Poplar Field (WC)

Fugitive farewells now felled—
durable shade fled them to
another retreat, whisper-
ing where hazels afford per-
ishing longer laid on leaves:
poplar lies screened, song's colonn-
ade its haste in cooler stead.

Apple Tree (JD)

A silent fashion of root
discovers no orchard spell
perturb its station's quiet
emboss, loud scent in blossom.
Wish it a patience hung with
song of apple-stain, deny
no shining content a rind.

The Willow (WD-L-M)

Sways mute memory: southern
in whisper the wind leans fair
until locked in swept willow.
Sighs with delicate lash a
sap of wintry green driven
by void of the leaf: parches
to a kiss midnight's upflow.

The Leafless Tree (BMD)

An unflinching semblance lies
unseen, inviolate for
transient, that bare shimmer
closely fallen. Ex-summer
claims congenial life on
leafless symbol, higher blown
earthward, green trapping outward.

Reciprocity (JD)

In my troubled constancy
I can wish wisdom daunted
fixity, and little think
envy widens moral skies
or composure quits silent
things invested in my cries:
peace a windless stir in trees.

An Elegy of Elms (ARF)

Homeward untimely laid home,
more borrowed than cool shade from
continuance: snow laden with
withering hosts a stick of
welcome. Elm greened with us be-
fore, then wove a tracery
of lanes leafless to amend.

Ode to a Tree (JG)

Throughout a dell's sympathy
the century of enough
branching tells of beaten trace,
of its erect inkling con-
cealing the tyranny of
brave weather: for none has stood
bitter to the times of leaf.

The Votive Tree (EG)

Gladdened by strange foliage
waking on rough branch, token
of a wind moved to death but
shaken with a sprawl of de-
plorable gift: wild olive
festoons seawood, batters ebb
as at fruit entered aware.

Elms (JG)

Too rare a barrier up-
lift wandering a small world's
too wild a void's quiet, made
kindly when cloud rarety
overwhelms shadowy drooping:
elms are a night circumfer-
ence of thought held free to set.

In a Wood (TH)

Poplar to oak cannot come.
Bough halts pine but lives out beech
in slim dream of sapling peace,
no tall release taught of trees.
A rival's touch of ease smiles
loyalties, city kin have
spun a nest to enter in.

Binsey Poplars (GMH)

Prick a country mended, hew
fresh comers from sandals they
quench, spare the rural leaping
in slender cage but rank an
after-aspen eye: selves of
havoc quell a hack green, delve
tender in folded seeing.

Song of Poplars (AH)

Pierce blue rumour of the mute,
let sky tune hued silences,
spear into sunlight the mind's
twin, trembling leafage, unde-
fined stair of serene rift. A
whisper rusts shrillness upward,
springing gummed and blind as trees.

Magnolia (IJ)

Driven protectingly, tent's
overshadow light as drift
ranged behind the blaze briefly
withdrawn into blossom, snow
a sphere of level artless-
ness: unsullied paradise
lively for its aftermath.

The English Garden (WM)

Whose lessening free space drops
distinction, catches to bounds
a distant scene on a dark
curtain. Our eye gives alder
or cedar to the broads of
beech, the lofts of abele:
horizon has no lender.

Orchard Idyll (SM)

Arcaded glance from bough to
loft, no break in crests of spring
where orchard passes last to
sea, a spread of fragile surf
sailing separately the
russet skies: green globes prison
steep in the appointed row.

Dirge in the Woods (GM)

Glow, pine-tree, but not a drop
on the lives of roots, clouding
a sea of lines as if the
sway were still overhead. Go
quiet, mosses, under chase.
Wild flooring rushes its dead,
even we fruit at the race.

Lines Written on an August Morning (JMM)

An untasted tree, flagged by
the soul dreaming anodyne
islands, sails a forgotten
toll, weeps pride for barren tide.
Unvintaged by uplift where
dust on lip is vainly first:
a tree shipped will drop its thirst.

Tree Planting (AN)

That guessed parts eye the love we
took to its own tree-pause, then
plant well the storm in its place
on a hill of vanished spot.
Every knoll shall stand playing
landscape against lovely fill,
true pains give when we are gone.

The Scotch Fir (WHO)

Tallest stir within bleak lean
of stoop, light-leaved than glare summ-
er from branch: whether my worst
world stand forth greenly yoked to
storm, but stemmed at the mood of
feet under woods, interlude
of roots rough among bracken?

Song of Palms (AO'S)

Shock broken by untraversed
hollow, its blaze might close that
ripe feud fed equal flower,
zone-explosion in an un-
replying bower. Long change
which a palm-like reach lulled, scant
wave binds as a green flaunt sheds.

In the Beechwood (JDCP)

Swayed hidden without the wood's
full swerve, silence only as
straight cloud pillars it rose-bare
across small uneasy sun,
erect green still wintry in
air: grey branches' unashamed
dim highest assured of pause.

Poplars (MP)

Burn all flutter in tall breeze,
fight poplar democracies
in each border candle, un-
clouded where other trees bend
truth reedy, turning wars free
in heaven: you tower the
trammel of a common wood!

Hawthorns (DUR)

Plain stranger-plenty, I put
in rowans homed between twen-
ty hawthorns, each sapling trav-
els a lilt given ruby
or berried inches, branches
thorned for finches far too tall
to wing time out of feat leaves.

The Trees of the Garden (DGR)

Blind boughs shrink supremacy
where that silent yoke, shall cease
standing haggard faced with known
sapling depth. Roots look past om-
inous clustering, invoke
a wisp showing in trees, un-
abashed hillock of walled storm.

Trees (MS)

Reserved homage angry in
shank of branching it poor, a
monotone uplift prints cones
quite at home for treeless com-
pany, enduring the clue
of hedge, locked thin but ever-
green in no dictated soil.

The Cuckoo Wood (EBS)

Scarce cuckoo so to renew,
rooting disfavour, you lift
high lair when undone. Treas-
ured spears unregarded wane
in pride of outward under-
wood: filters a green circle
round that cause for company.

Outlived by Trees (SS)

Tree by when, a beech or lime
grows me or you. You'll stand
time for me while cedars sur-
vive in green what a lifetime
teaches last: a share of trans-
ience limes the dead, lawns a
shadow body past its tree.

A Hollow Elm (ES)

Soft-riven wood not cheated
not withstood, a tempest stands
in you unmocked, gapes warm op-
en pollard, with first light lives
so hollow: transience sweet-
ened ancient sides, new sun sent
stiffly out at soft spring's beck.

The Tree Uprooted (DSS)

Branches die—a garment in
prison flight, death silences
the wind's place for a bondage
in clad air. It snows exile
where leaves fought the last tilling
earth allows: greenwood at rest
trails its manifold alone.

Copper Beeches (KS)

Today shadows pasture a
high beech shoulder, stain bliss at
crimson window whose green thought
saw glass feathered on leaves with
translucent forestallings: type
slender sunwhite for flame-scrap,
copper it from heaven's crust.

The Holly Tree (RS)

Whose nothing to wound is gloss
on unarmed graze, apt prickle
intrudes abroad its grave throng,
chance emblem at home to points
circling intelligent asp-
erities: keen leaves show fear
of harshness tempers winter.

The Silent Trees (JS)

The scattered quiet is guessed
concourse, tired flooded silence
entangled for an outpost
of calm stem stilled into stream:
obscurely caught easing an
untaught death, bound moves nothing
taller than tree fielding sky.

Aspens (ET)

Save random winter out of
footless cavern of wind, what-
ever ceaseless shoe of leaf
furs that bare anvil once moon-
light: aspens talk grieving shop,
cross tempest's reasonable
drowning by ghosting their house.

The Yew Tree (ALT)

Which sun grasps at the tree's name
fibres of a sullen first-
ling, which season of a thous-
and dusks brands the dreamless glows
of men? Yew, you flower summ-
er nets of root failing to
wrap the bloom incorporate.

The Tree (EU)

Break roots to a summer of
need, fulfilled pilgrim greened to
reluctance. Corrosive surr-
enders are a scabbard roam-
ing the shielding, maternal
heir to maiden bough-stretch: danced
paths hush your wintry effort.

The Timber (HV)

Groves break to showers beneath
skies lightly dead, storm-flourish
of thriving line. Bright bowers
dissent at root, resentment
not to waste succession.
Green dreams lodge enduring temp-
est, shine for fierce, senseless rest.

Winter Branches (AV)

No one denudes marvel, no
one is oak's tall winter as
life's bare standing undoffed robs
custom of blind surprise. Prick
oak to skeleton of strange
resign, its annual pall-
ing not as it should not be.

Song of the Redwood-Tree (WW)

Fateful haunts, neighbouring strong
fading: palpable its deep
shanty future hears might's dense
dying. And riven saline
with ears of a sea's axes,
the forest shore is stalwart,
a refrain joined giant-low.

Yew Trees (WW)

To be disturbed upcoiling
fraternal, unrejoicing
scattered over the natu-
al, sheddings uninformed grass-
less: too slow to furnish the
festal intertwist, but liv-
ing crossed notes of things pillared.

SALT POETS

Robert Adamson
Adam Aitken
Louis Armand
Douglas Barbour
Andrea Brady
Pam Brown
Andrew Burke
Andrew Duncan
John Forbes
Dennis Haskell
Lyn Hejinian
Michael Hulse
S. K. Kelen
John Kinsella
Peter Larkin
Anthony Lawrence
Sophie Levy

Kate Lilley
Leo Mellor
Anna Mendelssohn
Rod Mengham
Drew Milne
Peter Minter
Simon Perril
Hilda Raz
Peter Riley
Gig Ryan
Tracy Ryan
Phil Salom
Susan M. Schultz
Tom Shapcott
Keston Sutherland
John Tranter
Susan Wheeler

www.ingramcontent.com/pod-product-compliance
Lightning Source LLC
Chambersburg PA
CBHW022005090426
42741CB00007B/903